THE ABBEY OF THE HOLY GHOST

Margaret of York, Charles the Bold,
and the Politics of Devotion

Kathryn Anderson Hall, PhD

ARCHWAY
PUBLISHING

Archway Publishing books may be ordered through booksellers or by contacting:

Archway Publishing
1663 Liberty Drive
Bloomington, IN 47403
www.archwaypublishing.com
1 (888) 242-5904

ISBN: 978-1-4808-7328-5 (sc)
ISBN: 978-1-4808-7329-2 (e)

Library of Congress Control Number: 2018915055

Print information available on the last page.

Archway Publishing rev. date: 4/16/2019

For Richard
and our family

CONTENTS

CONTEXTUAL INTRODUCTION

The house of memory metaphor for prompting one's ordered recall has its oldest surviving treatment of the subject in the Pseudo-Ciceronian *Rhetorica ad Herennium* (3.xvi.28 – xxiv.40). By setting the lawyer's memorized speech against the familiar background and visual images of entering and walking through a house enabled the speaker to initiate and progress through his set-speech in its public performance. Chaucer's *Troilus and Criseyde* (V.528 ff.)—"And to Criseydes hous they gonnen wende"—notably dramatizes the metaphor to prompt Troilus' memory of his beloved. The longest and most famous expression of the technique is Guillaume de Lorris and Jean de Meun's *Roman de la Rose* where the house is transformed into a garden inhabited by the lover, his metaphorical beloved rose, and the psycho-analytical constituents of the loving process. *L'Abbaye du Saint Esprit* and its Middle English articulation *The Abbey of the Holy Spirit* follows in this long-standing and successful tradition of organization to lift the composition off the page and into the memory. The central metaphor of the abbey has precedents in Hugh of St.-Victor's *De claustro animae*, Aelred of Rievaulx's sermon on the text *Intravit Jesus in quoddam castellum* (Luke 10:38), for the feast of the Assumption, Mechtild of Magdeburg's cloister of the virtues, and Robert Grosseteste's *Templum Domini*, which also found its own Middle English expression in verse.

The Abbey / *L'Abbaye* begins in the setting of the Conscience which needs cleansing by Righteousness and Love of Purity. Then Meekness and Poverty lay the foundation along the River of Tears or Repentance. Obedience and Pity raised the walls of alms with the cement of Love-of-God and Steadfast Faith. Forbearance and Strength place the pillars. The chapter house, refectory, chapel, dormitory, infirmary, cellar, and storeroom have their individual patrons in the construction. The warden and visitor (Holy Ghost), abbess (Charity), prioress (Wisdom), sub-prioress (Meekness), treasurer (Discretion), preceptor (Prayer), cellarer (Devotion), and cook (Penance) are all accounted for—the last perhaps with a touch of irony. Temperance, Prayer, Devotion, et al., find their appointed duties. Finally, a tyrant, the devil, came with his four daughters (Envy, Pride, Complaint, and Judging-Others-Unjustly) to lodge by force. The chapel bell is rung and counsel is sought. The *Veni Creator Spiritus* is sung and the Holy Ghost expels the tyrant's daughters. You[1] are advised to follow the good habits of these ladies and keep the fiend's four daughters from your hearts.

The preceding thirteenth and fourteenth century settings for memory to the late seventeenth century allegorical road map by John Bunyan's *Pilgrim's Progress from This World, to That Which Is to Come* is conceptually only a short stroll along an English footpath. But the metaphors in *Troilus, Roman,* or *Abbey/Abbaye* are recognizable as having their origin in classical Roman training for the public address. It is an effective method by which to organize our own journey through law, love, or devotion.

Concerning *Ha Fille*[2]

The recurring use of the vocative *Ha Fille* in *The Abbey of the Holy Ghost* comes out of a rich tradition of the hortatory, the allegorical, and the direct address to the audience employed in the Scriptural Canticle of Canticles and the plethora of medieval commentaries applied to that most memorable book of the Old Testament.

In the Scriptures women become noticed primarily for their relationships to men. The book of Ruth celebrates the life of a widow. Judith follows a woman warrior and her exploits. Esther is a maiden who has her fifteen minutes of fame with (Arta)xerxes. The Canticle of Canticles allows us to glimpse a woman in the only elements allowed to her in antiquity—her sexuality and her love life. It was natural that the Canticles became the archetype by which the medieval Church could speak to women.

It is only in the Canticles that the depiction of a woman is enticing as a

---

[1] The readers.

[2] *Ha Fille* in *The Abbey of the Holy Ghost* translates to "Listen, Daughter" and was ostensibly used to address the soul of the reader. In some cases, it could also address a particular reader herself.

person who uses her womanliness in liberty and freedom. Small wonder that the Canticles were co-opted by men for their own purposes in commentaries. Among the Latins there is Ambrose's frequent use of the Canticles. Three commentaries by Gregory the Great demonstrate its attraction. The Venerable Bede composed a number of smaller commentaries. The exposition by Honorius of Autun in its historical, allegorical, tropological, and anagogical meanings takes it into another dimension. The eighty-six sermons by St. Bernard were commonly known in the medieval period. The Canticle of Canticles enkindled love for God on the theme of affection between a man and a woman (literal or historical meaning); Christ and his bride, the Church (allegorical); God and the soul (tropological); and the Word and human nature (anagogical).

In the Canticles of the Vulgate the word *filia* "daughter" occurs uniformly in a context: *inter filias* "among the daughters," *filias Jerusalem (Sion)* "the daughters of Jerusalem (Sion)," *filia principis* "O prince's daughter," and *filiæ multitudinis* "daughter of the multitude." Elsewhere in the Canticles the feminine principle is analyzed as *sponsa* "spouse," *adolescentulæ* "young maidens," *soror "sister,"* etc. The Latin allows the delineation of the feminine unlike the translation: *Quam pulchra es, et quam decora, carissima* "How beautiful art thou, and how comely, my dearest." The diverse presentations of the feminine principle in the Canticles inspired in the Commentators their own extensions of female prerogatives to yet further figurative applications.

The diversity of the rights, charms, and prerogatives of women as exemplified in the Canticles and its commentaries stirred the writers of mystical allegories to apply a similar abundance of personifications to their narratives. The recurring use of the vocative *Ha Fille* in the *L'Abbaye du saint esprit / The Abbey of the Holy Ghost* comes out of this fertile tradition of the hortatory, the allegorical, and the direct address to the audience. The frequency and placement of *Ha Fille* awakens the listener to crucial junctures in the narrative just as the different uses of *filia* in the Canticles. In the context of the virtues as feminine in the *Abbaye/Abbey* the use of *Ha Fille* speaks to the women addressed just as lovingly as the woman in the Canticles.

Eugene J. Crook, Emeritus Professor of English
Florida State University

CHAPTER 1

L'ABBAYE DU SAINT ESPRIT:[3]
INFLUENCES AND ATTRIBUTIONS

L'Abbaye du saint esprit is a medieval devotional treatise written for those who "would like to enter into religion but may not"[4] for various reasons. The treatise seeks to aid the uncloistered reader in living a spiritual life by creating, within the reader's conscience, a metaphorical abbey in which each room represents a Christian virtue or a charitable act. After meditating on the metaphorical abbey, a devout person could symbolically carry its spiritual lessons out into the secular world. In living this "mixed life"[5] of spiritual contemplation and charitable actions, a spiritual person could bring together the seemingly opposed lifestyles of withdrawing from the world while living fully in it.

The *L'Abbaye du saint esprit* begins its early life in France from at least the early 14th century and later crosses the Channel into England some sixty years later. Currently, the *L'Abbaye du saint esprit* exists in eleven Old and Middle French manuscripts dating from 1300,[6] while twenty-four Middle English

---

[3] *The Abbey of the Holy Spirit.* Middle English versions of the treatise are referred to as *The Abbey of the Holy Ghost.*

[4] That is, they would like to join a religious order but cannot because they are married, do not have a "dowry," or have another conflict. Translation (mine) of 14th century Royal 16E.XII French redaction of the text: "Voudroient entre en religion et ne pueent," Royal 16E.XII (f. 132, l. 8). The later English Thornton Ms, refers to those who "walde be in religyone but þay may noughte," (f. 21, l.3).

[5] A life in which a person does not take religious vows but lives spiritually as a nun or priest might within the secular world.

[6] *Catalogue of Additions to the Manuscripts in the British Museum, 1854-1860* (London: The Trustees of the British Museum, 1965), 211. See the Bibliography for a listing of all known English and French manuscripts of *L'Abbaye du saint esprit.* Janice Pinder of Monash University

manuscripts exist with the earliest possible date for the English treatises being 1358.[7] Clearly a popular treatise in the fourteenth and fifteenth centuries, the earliest (from c. 1300) French redactions of *L'Abbaye du saint esprit* feature the narrative framework of the allegorical abbey without the more mystical material found in later texts. Later French manuscripts[8] present longer, much-elaborated versions of the treatise, while the Douce 365 and its "sister manuscript," Vesoul 91 include an additional direct address of *Fille* (Daughter) and a 352-line dialogue between *Fille* and Christ not present in any other redaction of the treatise. Among the French texts of *L'Abbaye*, the fourteenth-century Royal 16E.XII presents the redaction closest to the later English versions, while Douce 365 and Vesoul 91 represent the only French texts to contain the distinctive conclusion of the later English treatises. Such textual connections between the English and French treatises argue for a complex relationship between the French and English versions of *L'Abbaye* that appears to be more organic than linear in development.

A close study of the important redactions of *L'Abbaye du saint esprit* confirms Jerome McGann's view of literary work as a "cultural product" which disperses authority beyond the text itself, especially in the case of multiple authors, as is the case with this treatise.[9] According to McGann, the "complex network of people, material and events that produces literary works and continues to influence them may assist in the understanding of …social and historical patterns."[10] Certainly, such a complex network influenced the Douce 365 version of *L'Abbaye du saint esprit* commissioned by the English Princess Margaret of York for her upcoming marriage in 1469 to Charles the Bold, Duke of Burgundy. The present study will focus on the political events, religious

---

has located two fifteenth-century redactions of the *L'Abbaye* in the Latin manuscripts BNF 2095 and BNF 19397 that appear to belong to a later date than the ones examined in this study. See Janice Pinder, "Love and Reason from Hugh of Fouilloy to the *Abbaye du saint esprit*: Changes at the Top in the Medieval Cloister Allegory, *Parergon*, 27 (2010), 67-83.

[7] Peter Consacro. *"The Author of The Abbey of the Holy Ghost from All Known Extant English Manuscripts with Introduction, Notes, and Glossary.* Diss. (Fordham, 1971. Ann Arbor: UMI, 1971), xc.

[8] The fourteenth-century Royal 16E.XII and fifteenth-century Douce 365.

[9] Jerome McGann, *A Critique of Modern Textual Criticism* (Chicago: U of Chicago P,1985), 84.

[10] McGann, "The Monks and the Giants," *Textual Criticism and Literary Interpretation* (Chicago: U of Chicago P, 1985), 193.

and economic forces, and significant people that gave rise to the formation of the Douce 365 French treatise as compared with earlier redactions, while also considering elements of audience and social context that might have shaped significant emendations.

Early Contexts and the Building of the Metaphorical Abbey

It is significant that *L'Abbaye du saint esprit* evolves as a text during centuries fraught with challenges to traditional religious belief. The oldest extant French manuscript, Yates Thompson 11, follows more than two hundred years after the eleventh-century reaction to the excesses of Carolingian monasticism that existed in contrast to the simple piety of the apostolic church,[11] and certain redactions of the treatise reflect the twelfth- to thirteenth-century rise in clerical power and the accompanying appreciation and concern that attended it.[12] *L'Abbaye du saint esprit* continued to develop during the fourteenth century which witnessed the plague of 1348 that decimated at least a quarter to a third of the population of Europe as well as the Great Western Schism which, at one point, saw three popes reigning simultaneously.[13] During times of social and religious upheaval, the treatise survived to call the faithful to embody more fully the love of Christ at the same time that it expressed concern over the corruption in the institutional church that eroded public confidence.[14] A popular treatise, *L'Abbaye du saint esprit* encouraged devout individuals to practice an affective religion of interiority that sought to bring them into meaningful contact with the Divine and their neighbors. The accompanying desire of believers for a more

---

[11] See C.H. Lawrence, *Medieval Monasticism* (London: Longman, 2001), 286-288; Christiana Whitehead, "Making a Cloister of the Soul in Medieval Religious Treatises," *Medium Aevum* 67 (1998), 4; and *L'Abbaye du saint esprit*, Ms. Douce 365, f. 169v, ll. 14,15 for the change in the mortar holding the abbey together from "living faith" to "true faith."

[12] See Carolyn Walker Bynum, *Jesus as Mother* (Berkeley: U of California P, 1982), 14-21.

[13] The Great Schism lasted from 1378 to 1417. See Renate Blumenfeld-Kosinski for the artistic and visionary responses to the Great Western Schism. R. Blumenfeld-Kosinski, *Poets, Saints, and Visionaries of the Great Schism, 1378-1417.* University Park: Penn State U P, 2006.

[14] See Malcolm Lambert, *Medieval Heresy: Popular Movements from the Gregorian Reform to the Reformation* (Malden, MA: Blackwell, 2002), 239-246, 323-349, 392-414.

immediate relationship with God that arose during this period did not preclude participation in institutional religion; rather, it took place as an adjunct to it and often enhanced the individual spiritual experience during Mass.[15]

By c.1358, *The Charter of the Abbey of the Holy Ghost* followed the Middle English treatise of *The Abbey of the Holy Ghost* in Ms. Winchester College 33. A work of a completely different nature than *The Abbey, The Charter of the Abbey of the Holy Ghost* has been found by N.F. Blake, Carl Horstmann, and Clara Fanning to have been written by a different author and with a content that demonstrates little relation to its predecessor.[16] For his part, N.F. Blake finds *The Charter* to be "almost certainly the work of another author despite the texts' amalgamation in the de Worde editions and in some manuscripts."[17] Horstmann states that *The Charter* is "the work of another author,"[18] and Clara Fanning notes the lack of a relationship between *The Charter* and *The Abbey* by affirming the absence of a French original, the staunch anonymity of the text, and its paucity of devotional fervor.[19] Hope Emily Allen asserts that *The Charter* is written by a person without "mystical interests,"[20] and Julia Boffey notes that *The Charter* is "couched in terms of a legal document" and that this legal format "seems to relate in some way to the various charters of Christ that proliferated in Middle

---

[15] See Eamon Duffy, *The Stripping of the Altars: Traditional Religion in England 1400-1580* (New Haven: Yale U P, 2005), 92-95. While discussing the veneration of the Host during the fifteenth century, Duffy notes that with the affective response, the Host became "far more than the object of individual devotion [but also became] a means of forgiveness and sanctification: It was the source of human community" (93).

[16] According to Curt F. Buhler's study for the Bibliographical Society of the University of Virginia, the earliest of de Word's editions was printed in 1496 and is housed in the Pierpont Morgan Library (106). C.F. Buhler, "The First Edition of "The Abbey of the Holy Ghost." *Studies in Bibliography*, 6 (1953-54), 101-06

[17] N.F. Blake, Trans. *Middle English Religious Prose* (London: Billing & Sons, 1972), 88.

[18] C. Horstmann. *Yorkshire Writers: Richard Rolle of Hampole and His Followers.* (London: Swan Sonnenschein, 1895), 321.

[19] Clara Elizabeth Fanning. *The Charter of the Abbey of the Holy Ghost: A Critical Edition from All Known Extant Manuscripts with Introduction, Notes, and Glossary.* Diss. (Fordham, 1975. Ann Arbor: UMI, 1975).

[20] Hope Emily Allen. *Writings Ascribed to Richard Rolle, Hermit of Hampole, and Materials for His Biography.* (New York: Heath, 1927), 337

English."[21] Boffey concludes that the "most striking feature" of *The Charter* and *The Abbey*, taken together, lies in "their ready adaptability to the needs of late-medieval readers of all kinds, and their capacity to be reshaped and redefined according to various contingencies."[22] *The Charter* and *The Abbey* were probably conflated due to similarity of material and name, an idea strengthened by Winken de Worde's decision to print them together in one highly popular volume in the fifteenth century.

Arriving in England at a time when lay piety was gaining momentum, *The Abbey of the Holy Ghost* also enjoyed widespread popularity as evidenced by its presence in twenty-four extant Middle English manuscripts. The English treatises which derived from the French tradition were used by both men and women in private devotions, and in so doing, served by its wide distribution to extend the influence of the monastery into daily life through the reinforcement of monastic virtues and charitable acts. For this reason, Nicole R. Rice views *L'Abbaye du saint esprit* as a work that aids "readers in the attainment of 'symbolic capital'" (225) through the attainment of "spiritual ambition," a phrase she defines as "the desire for the highest distinctions in the religious realm…" (224).[23] For all its encouragement of individual affective devotion, the treatise does not appear to have threatened the spiritual influence of the institutional church.[24]

For its part, *The Abbey of the Holy Ghost,* in its French and English versions, is not strictly a mystical text that instructs the reader via specific steps leading toward union with God as in Marguerite Porete's *Mirror of Simple Souls* or Walter Hilton's *Scale of Perfection*. It is a contemplative text that constructs an allegorical abbey in the conscience through the use of metaphorical "stones" made up of charitable acts and of monastic virtues, such as Patience, Strength, Mercy, Obedience, and Poverty. In this capacity, *L'Abbaye du saint esprit* seeks to inculcate monastic values in the lay reader while serving as an aid to meditation.

---

[21] Julia Boffey, "*The Charter of the Abbey of the Holy Ghost* and Its Role in Manuscript Anthologies," *The Yearbook of English Studies,* 33 (2003): 120, 122.

[22] Boffey, 130.

[23] Nicole R. Rice. "Spiritual Ambition and the Translation of the Cloister: *The Abbey* and *Charter of the Holy Ghost.*" *Viator: Medieval and Renaissance Studies.* 33 (2002): 222-260.

[24] As Eamon Duffy implies, private affective devotions often served to reinforce Church teachings among committed Christians. See Duffy, 93.

The earliest French version, Yates Thompson 11, begins with the purging of the conscience by Truth and Love of Purity, followed by the construction of the abbey's foundations by Humility and Poverty. Obedience and Mercy then raise the walls of the abbey, while Patience and Strength set up the pillars that support them. The abbey is founded on a river of tears, recalling the remorse of Mary Magdalene, the river that makes glad the city of God in Psalm 45,[25] and the river of God that produces abundance in Psalm 64.[26] The river of tears in the fifteenth-century Douce 365 *L'Abbaye* reflects the emphasis on penitence set forth by the Fourth Lateran Council in 1215 and leads the reader into a deeper spiritual commitment by emphasizing "good works for the love of God" and almsgiving to increase the number of "good stones we put in our edifice and in our wall."[27] The construction of the abbey continues with help from Patience and Strength, and is followed by both a stricture advising containment and by architectural metaphors that emphasize Compassion and Devotion. Charity becomes the abbess, while Wisdom acts as prioress; Discretion, Prayer, Devotion, Penitence, Reason, and Largess all have duties in the abbey as do Meditation, Devotion, and Jealousy (who guards the entire edifice).

The French Royal 16E.XII and Douce 365 treatises include a meditation on the Eucharist, while the Douce 365 redaction also includes an additional and lengthy meditation between Christ and the Soul, addressed to *Fille* (Daughter), not found in other redactions of the text. At the end of this redaction, the four daughters of hell – Envy, Pride/Presumption, Murmur/Detraction, and False Judgment of Others – disturb the abbey's peace, necessitating the saving intervention of the

---

[25] "The stream of the river maketh the city of God joyful: the most High hath sanctified his own tabernacle. God is in the midst thereof, it shall not be moved: God will help it in the morning early" (Psalm 45:5-6). The stream, in this case, is "glad" because of the role of remorse in leading one to repentance and forgiveness of sin. The *Douay Rheims Bible* is used for English scriptural notations throughout this study; Latin scripture in the parallel texts is referenced using a translation of Jerome's Latin Vulgate Bible.

[26] "Thou hast visited the earth, and hast plentifully watered it: thou hast many ways enriched it. The river of God is filled with water: thou hast prepared their food; for so is its preparation" (Psalm 64:10).

[27] "...bon[n]es oeuvres que nous faisons pour lamour de dieu par son co[m]mandement" (Douce 365, f. 2, ll. 26-27 – f. 2v, l. 1.) "Et quantes aulmosnes que [nous] donnons autant de bonnes pieres mettons nous en n[ot]re edifice et en nostre mur" (Douce 365, f. 2v, ll. 2-4).

Holy Spirit, who is informed of the discord by Charity, Wisdom, and Humility. The abbey is restored, stronger than ever, and the later French treatises end with a warning to guard one's spiritual life carefully, an admonition of heightened significance when the specified reader neither inhabits an actual abbey nor is bound by the formal vows of a specific religious order.

Victorine Influences and Possible Attributions

The treatise, in both French and English, owes an early debt of influence to the Victorine School established outside of Paris in the early twelfth century and to *devotio moderna*, a movement that emphasized personal virtue and con-templation.[28] The Victorines, as Canons Regular, concerned themselves with contemplation, mysticism, scholarship, and service, while emphasizing commu-nal life, the ineffable mystery of God, and the manifestation of the Spirit in all things.[29] These elements can be seen in French and English versions of *L'Abbaye du saint esprit* with their emphasis on meditation, encouragement of charitable acts, and specific references to scriptural and patristic works. Indeed, so strong is this correlation that early attributions, which have since fallen into disfavor, credited Hugh of St. Victor with authorship of the treatise despite the absence of a Latin original.[30]

The authorial attribution to Hugh of St. Victor also had at its core the prelate's monastic reading model which favored visual mnemonics to impart intangible ideas. In his *Didascalicon*, Hugh advocates a method of analysis that begins with tangible, finite objects and progresses to the intangible and "infinite" (or

---

[28] *Devotio moderna* especially influences the later (French) Douce 365 *L'Abbaye*.

[29] See Steven Chase, *Contemplation and Compassion* (Maryknoll, NY: Orbis, 2003), 15-25.

[30] The dates of Hugh of St. Victor's life and those of the earliest manuscripts do not correspond: Hugh lived c.1096-1141 and the earliest manuscript (the Yates Thompson Ms. 11) has been dated to c. 1300, as stated above. A Latin manuscript for *L'Abbaye du saint esprit* has not been found, although Horsmann mentions a Latin treatise entitled *Abbacia de S. Spiritu* (321). As that manuscript is now lost, however, it is difficult to ascertain if that treatise contains parallels with the French *L'Abbaye du saint esprit*. Claims for Richard Rolle's authorship of *The Abbey of the Holy Ghost* in English cannot be maintained as that work is most certainly taken from the French manuscripts which predate Rolle by some 300 years.

"undefined") abstractions.[31] In this process, he suggests starting with "history" first (in Christian devotional works, this often involves scripture, especially the story of Christ's life, death, and resurrection) and then moving to the allegorical construction of a building or other mnemonic structure that would allow the reader to "gather brief and dependable abstracts to be stored in the little chest of the memory...."[32] The ultimate goal of such a project lay in restoring the integrity of human nature – that immortal part of a person that exists eternally – through knowledge and the attainment of virtue.[33]

Scripture, according to Hugh of St. Victor, is best contemplated as a building, with a foundation based upon history, a structure built stone by stone according to guiding principles, and an ultimate meaning that has tropological implications. Hugh advised that the reader

> ...lay first the foundation of history; next, by pursuing the 'typ-
> ical' meaning, build up a structure in [the] mind to be a fortress
> of faith. Last of all, however, through the loveliness of morality,
> paint the structure over as with the most beautiful of colors.[34]

Hugh further elaborates the principles of "true faith" that guide the metaphorical construction and emphasizes the profundity of thought gained through meditation by which one "investigates the mysteries of allegories."[35] The use of a similar rhetorical model in *L'Abbaye du saint esprit* no doubt led to the ascription of the work to Hugh of St. Victor, even though the use of architectural metaphor is widespread in medieval treatises and is not, in itself, an adequate indication of provenance.[36]

The erroneous ascription to Hugh of St. Victor may have arisen, additionally,

---

[31] Hugh of St. Victor. *The Didascalicon of Hugh of Saint Victor.* Trans. Jerome Taylor (New York: Columbia U P, 1991), 92.

[32] Hugh, 94.

[33] See Hugh, 51-52.

[34] Hugh, 138. Hugh owes a debt here to Gregory the Great, *Moralium libri* Epistula missoria III (PL, LXXV, 513C).

[35] Hugh, 139.

[36] Jerome Taylor notes that Philo of Alexandria wrote "Allegory is 'a wise architect who directs the superstructure built upon a literal foundation'" (p. 223, n. 14). Taylor finds this quotation

from confusion with Hugh of Fouilloy's *De claustro Animae*,[37] a work which resembles *L'Abbaye du saint esprit* in its use of architectural metaphor to relate spiritual actions and virtues within an easily memorable format. As with *L'Abbaye du saint esprit, De claustro animae* presents specific monastic spaces in conjunction with spiritual acts and virtues, such as meditation, compassion, and prayer, while it also considers the cloister in detail, explicating each of its four walls in relation to specific virtues.[38] Christiania Whitehead notes that this emphasis on the cloister evidences concern with "the contemplative condition of the soul,"[39] a characteristic emphasis of the Victorine school, as indicated above. This particular contemplative concern, however, remains an activity central to most, if not all, monastic orders.[40]

It is consequently difficult to ascertain who the original writer of this treatise might have been for several reasons. First, Hugh of St. Victor and Hugh of Fouilloy were roughly contemporary, both living in the twelfth century, while our earliest extant version of *L'Abbaye du saint esprit* dates from c.1300 and, as mentioned, no Latin original of the treatise has yet been found. Next, several biblical structures and theological works could have influenced the allegorical use of an abbey, including Solomon's temple, the Ark of the Covenant, Bede's *De Templo*,[41] and Augustine's *Civitatus Dei*. Scripture also provides a wealth of references that could have inspired an allegorical abbey, such as the city of God in Psalm 45,[42] the New Jerusalem of Revelation, and numerous references to God as refuge, fortress, and citadel.[43] Further, medieval mnemonics encouraged the

---

in Beryl Smalley, *The Study of the Bible in the Middle Ages* (New York: Philosophical Library, 1952), 5, where it is cited without reference.

[37] Whitehead, 5.

[38] See Whitehead, pp. 5-6, for a brief discussion of *De Claustro Anime*.

[39] Whitehead, 5.

[40] Carolyn Walker Bynum discusses the difficulty of distinguishing between monastic and other orders, particularly the canons regular, in her chapter on "The Spirituality of Regular Canons in the Twelfth Century" in *Jesus as Mother* (Los Angeles: U of California P, 1982), 22-58.

[41] These are also mentioned in Whitehead's discussion, p. 2.

[42] Psalm 45 in the Douay Rheims is listed as Psalm 46 in the King James Version. This river of the city in Psalm 46 (KJV) is also cited by N.F. Blake, p. 90.

[43] A few of these references include Ps. 30:3, Ps. 26:5, Ps. 18:3, Ps. 70:3, Jer. 16:19.

categorization of knowledge into readily usable systems that often emphasized the building of structures. Hugh of St. Victor, in his *Noah's Ark,* encourages the building of an edifice for God in one's heart:

> Now, therefore, enter your own inner-most heart, and make a dwelling-place for God. Make Him a temple, make Him a house, make Him a pavilion. Make Him an ark of the covenant, make Him an ark of the flood; no matter what you call it, it is all one house of God.[44]

As Mary Carruthers notes in *The Book of Memory*, the ark of the covenant or the ark of Noah was often allegorically represented as an *"arca sapientiae,"*[45] a collection of knowledge representing the wisdom one has gathered from study. Hugh of St. Victor describes this ark of wisdom as one of four to be built: "The third [ark] is [the one] wisdom builds daily in our hearts through continual meditation on the law of God."[46] The ark of wisdom, then, represents a categorized system of tropological information that one can readily recall as an aid in spiritual formation. While the structure of *L'Abbaye du saint esprit* reflects a similar purpose, the emphasis on a metaphorical abbey in *L'Abbaye du saint esprit* as a cloister of the soul renders the work one primarily concerned with individual, soulful contemplation.

A third ascription from the beginning of the Douce 365 *L'Abbey du saint esprit* links Jean Gerson, the Paris theologian, with the composition of the treatise: "Here begins a beautiful treatise formerly compiled by Master Jean Gerson, Doctor of Theology"(1.1).[47] With the earliest manuscript of *L'Abbaye du saint esprit*, Yates Thompson 11,[48] dating c.1300, it would, however, be impossible

---

[44] Hugh of St. Victor, *Fundamental Writings.* Vol. 2. Trans. Member of CSMV (USA: Revelation Insight, 2009), 80.

[45] "An ark of wisdom." Mary Carruthers, *The Book of Memory* (Cambridge, Cambridge U P, 1990), 43.

[46] Hugh of St. Victor, *Fundamental Writings*, 89. The other three arks include the one "which Noah made," the one that "Christ made" (the Church), and the one that "mother grace effects in us" (89).

[47] "Cy commence ung beau traittie jadis compile par maistre jehan jarson docteur en theologie."

[48] This manuscript was formerly known as the Additional Manuscript 39843.

for Gerson to have written the original treatise due to the dates in which he lived: 1363-1429. Further, the idea that he may be responsible for the additions and elaborations found in the Douce 365 *L'Abbaye*[49] that was commissioned by Margaret of York upon her marriage to Charles the Bold in 1468 also cannot be maintained. At best, perhaps Gerson's contemplative theology might have influenced some of the changes made by the Douce 365 scribe, David Aubert, to the earlier treatise found in the Royal 16 E.XII of the third redaction, as organized by Chesney.[50]

In a related attribution, Richard Rolle has received credit for the translation into English of *L'Abbaye du saint esprit*, based partly on the sole ascription of the work to him in the fifteenth-century Lambeth Palace Library 432 manuscript and carried forward by the affective language characteristic of Rolle found in that and other English versions.[51] In 1927, Hope Emily Allen countered this attribution in her *Writings Ascribed to Richard Rolle*, within a chapter entitled "Doubtful English Ascriptions."[52] She notes that the *Abbey*'s allegorical format is largely uncharacteristic of Rolle and is drawn from the French original, and concludes that it is "rash to conclude that Rolle was the translator of a widely distributed piece which is given to him in only one copy."[53] Many of the affective phrases which influenced the erroneous ascription to Rolle parallel French versions of the treatise and recall the flowering of mysticism on the continent as well as in England; they consequently are not necessarily a product of Rolleian influence. Perhaps Rosamund Allen is most accurate in noting that the "appeal to emotions"

---

[49] Chesney concludes that such an attribution may have been "an attempt to foist a work of unknown authorship on to an acknowledged authority on the spiritual life" (16). Kathleen Chesney. "Notes on Some Treatises of Devotion Intended for Margaret of York (Ms. Douce 365)." *Medium Aevum* 20 (1951): 11-39. The Vesoul 91 manuscript also contains this ascription in its *L'Abbaye*; yet, the Vesoul treatise exists within the same redaction as the Douce 365. Chesney finds it so similar to the Douce 365 treatise that she notes that the two versions contain the same "original hand" and "the same planning ...and [appear to have] emanated from the same workshop" (16).

[50] Chesney, 15.

[51] N.F. Blake mentions that the Lambeth version "is at best a translation from French by one of [Rolle's] followers" (88).

[52] H. E. Allen, 337.

[53] H. E. Allen, 343.

characteristic of devotional works after Anselm is "common to most spiritual writers," and in citing G. Liegey, that "[i]t seems hazardous to try to trace to any source the symbols of pilgrimage, betrothal, fire, song, light, sweetness, ascent, mountains, and wounds, for all of these seem common property to all who aspire to enter the [biblical] Holy City."[54]

The Incarnational Architecture of the Heart

Such a discrete visual mnemonic as a metaphorical abbey in one's conscience requires an emphasis on enclosure that exists from the earliest redaction of *L'Abbaye du saint esprit* found in the Yates Thompson 11 manuscript of c.1300. In each of the treatise's redactions, readers are reminded to guard their cloisters by controlling the senses if they truly wish to be religious, as is illustrated here in a passage from the Douce 365 *L'Abbaye*:

> Daughter, if you want to be truly religious, keep yourself closed and shut away, and thus you guard well your cloister. Lower and close your eyes and keep yourself from lightly looking, your ears from hearing evil about others, your mouth from speaking and laughing too much; close your heart against all evil thoughts. And [he] who guards himself well in these four ways, certainly he is quite religious.[55]

This admonition to enclosure carries with it a sense of urgency as uncloistered lay readers would work to achieve their spiritual goals without the communal and advisory structure of a religious order. Given the absence of this more formal support, it is understandable that the emphasis on enclosure and

---

[54] Rosamund Allen, "Introduction," *Richard Rolle: The English Writings* (New York: Paulist Press, 1988), 54.

[55] "Fille, se tu voeulz estre bien religieuse, tiens toy close et enfermee et ainsi tu gardes bien ton cloistre. Baisse et cloz tes yeulz et te obstiens de legierement regarder; tes oreilles du mal daultruy oyz; ton bouche de trop parler et rire. Cloz ton coeur encontre toute mauvaise pensee. Et qui bien se garde en ces quatre choses certes il est bien religieuz" (Douce 365, f. 3, ll. 15-22).

the ensuing reliance on the four cardinal virtues[56] occur early and unequivocally in the text. It is not, therefore, surprising, as Anne Savage and Nicholas Watson have remarked, that a similar concern with enclosure and discipline can be found in many religious texts meant for an individual audience, such as in the less sophisticated *Sawles Warde,* a thirteenth-century Middle English work in West Midlands dialect that forms part of the Katherine Group: "All the allegorical components of [*Sawles Warde]* – the body as the house or castle of the soul, the senses as its gates or guardians…and the four cardinal virtues – can easily be paralleled elsewhere."[57]

Disparate levels of language, formality, and complexity also distinguish *L'Abbaye du saint esprit* from the simple affective spirituality seen in the *herzklosterallegorien* motif used by the nuns of St. Walburg in medieval Germany.[58] The *herzklosterallegorien* focuses on individual devotion in which the contemplative's heart becomes the "cloister" in which her soul, during meditation, resides intimately with the Trinity. Jeffrey Hamburger finds the meditative art of the *herzklosterallegorien* to be closely related to *De Claustro animae,*[59] a treatise noted by Christiana Whitehead for its architectural allegory and parallels to *L'Abbaye du saint esprit.*[60] Hamburger, for his part, remarks on the popularity in Germany of works using architectural allegory,[61] one of which dates from 1454 and associates various virtues with particular aspects of monastic architecture.[62]

---

[56] Prudence, Temperance, Fortitude, Justice.

[57] Ann Savage and Nicholas Watson, Introduction to *Sawles Warde* in *Anchoritic Spirituality: Ancrene Wisse and Associated Works* (New York: Paulist P, 1991), 210. Aside from the setting of an abbey as opposed to a house, a major difference between *L'Abbaye du saint esprit* and *Sawles Warde* lies in the complexity and elegance of the former treatise in its later manifestations as opposed to the more down-to-earth simplicity of the much shorter *Sawles Warde.*

[58] The "heart as a cloister." See Jeffrey Hamburger's discussion of this image in *Nuns as Artists: The Visual Culture of a Medieval Convent* (New York: U of California P, 1997), 137-139.

[59] Jeffrey Hamburger, *Nuns as Artists,* 138 ff.

[60] Hamburger, 157; Hamburger attributes *De claustro animae* to John, prior of Saint-Jean-des Bignes near Soissons, while acknowledging that the work is "commonly attributed to Bernard of Clairvaux or Hugh of St. Victor…" (157).

[61] Ibid.

[62] Nuremberg, Stadtbibliothek, Ms Cent. VI, 43, ff. 196v-197r. This text comes from the Katharinenkloster in Nuremberg and is attributed textually to Bernard of Clairvaux. See Hamburger, p. 158, and n.63, p. 265.

This particular vernacular text discusses building the "spiritual monastery…in yourself," where "Humility is the prioress, Patience is the custodian, Mildness the director of the infirmary…."[63] The date of 1454 for this manuscript and the earlier date of 1300 for the French Yates Thompson 11 *L'Abbaye* argue for a dissemination of this devotional genre from France to Germany; however, it is possible an earlier treatise could have entered Germany from another source.[64]

In the homey art of the *hertzklostgerallegorien*, the "heart as a house," we see a similar, if far simpler, architectural and contemplative emphasis than that found in *L'Abbaye du saint esprit*. In one such artistic image from the convent of St. Walburg, a nun, within an allegorical heart, enjoys the embrace of Christ with the Father standing behind and over the couple, and with the Holy Spirit in the form of a dove looking on from its perch on Christ's knee. Rather poignantly, the portrayal of the nun and the Trinity in this simple domestic setting sublimates the natural desire for home and family to the nun's formal religious vows to her Beloved, Christ. The architecture of the heart here brings together the loving security of "home" within the containment of the cloister, as the "Fear of God," represented by the dog resting on the front stoop, guards the door to her heart.[65] The Lamb of God guards the opening of the chimney, and the Holy Spirit, in the form of a dove, looks on from his location near the window.[66] This scene,

---

[63] Ms. Cent. VI, 43, ff. 196v-197r, 1454, Stadtbibliothek, Nuremberg. (Quoted in Hamburger, p. 158; here I am using his translation.) G. Eis notes that the construction of the allegory varied according to the gender of the audience: in contrast to nuns, monks would have read that God is the abbot while discernment is the prior." See Eis in "Zwei unbekannte Handschriften der Allegorie vom Seelenkloster," *Leuvense Bijdragen* 53 (1964): 148-53. See Hamburger, n. 64, p. 265.

[64] A German treatise dating from 1407 states, "A peaceful heart is a spiritual monastery in which God himself is the abbot." The beginning of this treatise states that the monastery is built "according to the teaching of Saint Bernard." W. Stammler, in *Prosa der deutschen Gotik: Eine Stilgeschichte in Texten* (Berlin, 1933), Cat. No. 28, 50; qtd. in and trans. by Hamburger, p. 158.

[65] Hamburger, *Nuns as Artists*, 139. Of interest is a fifteenth-century altar cloth elaborately embroidered with a *hortus conclusus* representing the incarnation in which Mary is enclosed and Gabriel stands outside of the garden's gate blowing a horn and holding the leashes of four dogs representing Truth, Justice, Peace, and Mercy. See *Sur la Terre comme au ciel: Jardins d'Occident á la fin du Moyen Age.* (Paris: Musées nationaux, 2002), 58-59.

[66] Hamburger, 139. See Hamburger, pp. 137-144, for a discussion of enclosure and intimacy in this image.

touching in its everyday simplicity, captures the experience of mystical communion with the Trinity at the same time that it paints a picture of containment and domestic harmony. All of this occurs within the nun's heart and with clear appreciation for her sacred vows as the Bride of Christ. The domestic image is striking in its simplicity which sets it apart from the more formal perspective and language of of *L'Abbaye du saint esprit,* especially in the courtly redaction of the Royal 16E and Douce 365 manuscripts.

The Eucharistic aspect of mystical communion is particularly noticeable in another *herzklosterallegorien* image discussed by Hamburger.[67] In a second picture from St. Walburg, a nun sits at a Eucharistic banquet together with God, Christ, and the Holy Spirit, within the framework of a large heart that represents her own.[68] Again, the scene possesses a simplicity that suggests comfortable intimacy while painted in a vivid color and detail that witness to the importance of the spiritual metaphor to the cloistered artist herself. Christ has his arm around the nun's shoulders as if to present her to the Father,[69] the dove holds the chalice, and the Father prepares to distribute the host, while the nun treasures the mystical relationship within her heart.[70]

The transformational nature of the Eucharist reinforces these images as a study in the process of mystical embodiment, an incarnation of the Holy Spirit and of Christ in the individual believer that can become more apparent during a transcendent meditative experience. Similarly, *L'Abbaye du saint esprit* also represents an "incarnational" text, one that seeks to imbue the reader with a fuller awareness of the indwelling spirit of Christ and, therefore, aid in the reader's embodiment of the Divine. *L'Abbaye* differs from the *hertzklosterallegorien,*

---

[67] Hamburger, 140; see pp. 144ff. for Hamburger's discussion of the Eucharistic nature of this image.

[68] The heart is clearly that of the nun, rather than the Sacred Heart, as the dog, labeled as "Fear of God" guards the door to the heart, helping to maintain the spiritual enclosure necessary, by medieval standards, for maintaining such communion with the Divine. This same enclosure is emphasized in *L'Abbaye du saint esprit.* Hamburger, in *Nuns as Artists,* also does not see the heart of the Eucharistic feast as belonging to the tradition of the Sacred Heart of Jesus "with its less explicit mystical emphasis and its focus on the Passion, its exemplary emblem the *Cor Salvatoris"* (138).

[69] This gesture is noticed and discussed by Hamburger, p. 139.

[70] Luke 2:19.

however, in also focusing on the enforcement of specific moral strictures through meditation on Christian virtues. In asking the lay reader (of later redactions) to create an abbey in her heart to carry with her as she meditates on the virtues located within aspects of symbolic architecture, the treatise seeks to reinforce the construction of a temple not made by human hands, a living yet metaphorical abbey carried within the soul. This concept draws upon Paul's statement concerning the body as the temple of God in I Corinthians 3:16: "Know you not that you are the temple of God and that the Spirit of God dwelleth in you?"[71] In so doing, *L'Abbaye du saint esprit* challenges the reader to embody Christ and thereby participate in Divinity as it is made manifest in the world. Such an intimate manifestation foreshadows later mystical texts such as Theresa of Avila's *The Interior Castle.*

It is not surprising, then, that the frontispiece to the Yates Thompson 11[72] *L'Abbaye du saint esprit* contains an elaborate illustration in which the metaphorical ladies of the abbey, who represent allegorical virtues, appear in the garb of aristocratic women[73] and process within the architectural framework of the abbey[74] to celebrate the Eucharist.[75] In the lower register of the illustration, the nuns make their way through the abbey to the sanctuary, following their priest, the sacristan, and the cross. In the upper register, Mass has progressed to the point of transubstantiation at which time the bells are rung, and Christ appears above the altar surrounded by the banner, "ego sum vitis vera."[76] At this point, as

---

[71] Other scripture containing this idea includes I Cor. 3:17 and 6:19; II Cor. 6:16; Eph. 2:21; and Jer. 31:33. Henry Wansbrough, in the theological glossary appended to *The New Jerusalem Bible,* writes that "[t]he importance of the temple in Jerusalem was as the dwelling-place of God in the centre of his people. [T]he prophets taught that in the new covenant God would dwell in each individual heart, and Paul teaches that Christians are temples of the spirit" (168). The Douay-Rheims translation is used throughout for biblical quotations unless otherwise noted.

[72] Formerly Add. 39843.

[73] These ladies could also reflect the courtly readership for this treatise. (See cover illustration.)

[74] The abbey itself represents a more formal kind of *hertzklosterallegorien* as it is built within the reader's heart to be carried into the world.

[75] Yates Thompson 11 (London: British Library), fol. 6v.

[76] "I am the true vine." Jeffrey Hamburger describes the action in this illustration in *The Visual and the Visionary* and notes the architecture of enclosure that surrounds the nuns. See *The Visual and the Visionary: Art and Female Spirituality in Late Medieval Germany* (New York: Zone Books, 1998), 44.

Jeffrey Hamburger notes, the "lancets in the triforium [above the altar] double," drawing attention to this sacred space and the celebration taking place within it.[77] The emphasis on this corner of the illustration, its position at the highest interior point of the allegorical building and within the frame last viewed when reading left to right and bottom to top, secures the Eucharistic celebration with its sacred incarnational moment as the focal point of the work. This incarnation of the Divine within each believer underscores the main purpose of *L'Abbaye du saint esprit*: to nurture the spiritual within readers so that Christ may once again be embodied through their lives and actions. The abbey, representative of the "conscience" as mentioned within the Yates Thompson 11 manuscript, then, fulfills a similar role as the simple "heart as house" of the St. Walburg drawings: It seeks to nurture in the reader an indwelling, Christ-like spirit through contemplation, and encourage the subsequent practice of virtues and charitable acts as depicted by the allegorical nuns and architecture of the treatise.

While the frontispiece depicts a corporate form of worship that represents various spiritual practices helpful to the individual believer, a second illustration of the Yates Thompson 11 *L'Abbaye du saint esprit* focuses more singularly on the individual nun, her advisement and contemplation. As Jeffrey Hamburger notes in *The Visual and the Visionary,* the nun in the upper register meets with her advisor prior to praying at the altar of Mary's coronation, which represents "an exemplary model of the spousal state to which she aspires."[78] In the lower register, the same nun meditates on the Host in a profound contemplative moment which leads to her vision of Christ on the cross with the Father, arms outstretched, behind the Son. As Hamburger notices, there is no priest present during this moment of transcendence, highlighting the individual nature of this mystical experience.[79] This illustration portrays the individual affective experience which is preceded by sanctioned instruction and meditation as well as the nun's adoration and contemplation of the Eucharistic Host.

The frontispiece and this smaller image, taken together, emphasize the individual and transcendent nature of affective devotion while also confirming institutional oversight and participation. The metaphorical abbey with its allegorical

---

[77] Ibid.

[78] Hamburger, *Nuns as Artists,* 131.

[79] Ibid.

"ladies" becomes the City of God and a Temple of the Holy Spirit within the individual believer's heart, allowing the lay devout to live a consecrated life in the secular world after having experienced the ineffable sanctity of the Divine.

Relationships among the French Manuscripts

The French versions of *L'Abbaye du saint esprit* considered for this study confirm Kathleen Chesney's assertion that the treatise exists in four essential redactions.[80] The earliest redaction includes two manuscripts; of these, Add. 20697 closely follows Yates Thompson 11,[81] yet the former manuscript exists as a fragment and contains many abbreviations. The treatises of the second grouping, containing B.N.F. Nouv. Acq. 5232 (B.N.F. 5232) and Add. 29986, are almost identical, with some minor changes that make the B.N.F. 5232 version emerge as the smoother of the two. The now-lost Louvain treatise,[82] of which little is known, and the *L'Abbaye* of Royal 16E.XII constitute the third redaction of the text, with the latter manuscript embodying a courtly diction and style that reflects the aristocratic audience for which it was written. The fourth and final grouping includes the Douce 365 *L'Abbaye* commissioned by Margaret of York, Duchess of Burgundy, and the Vesoul 91 treatise. The first of these two manuscripts appears drawn from the Royal 16E.XII treatise and presents a more fully developed and sophisticated text than any found in the first three redactions. Chesney finds the Ms. Vesoul 91 *L'Abbaye* to be virtually identical to the Douce treatise yet lacking its artistic embellishments and illustrations. This difference leads Chesney to conclude that the Vesoul 91 *L'Abbaye* represents an "intermediate state [of the text]"[83] falling between the Royal 16E.XII and Douce 365 versions. She further states of the Vesoul and Douce treatises that it "seems

---

[80] Kathleen Chesney, "Notes on Some Treatises of Devotion Intended for Margaret of York (Ms. Douce 365)," *Medium Aevum* 20 (1951): 14. Janice Pinder of Monash University, Australia, located two copies of the *L'Abbaye* in Latin manuscripts BNF 2095 and BNF 19397. (See n. 5, p. 10.)

[81] Formerly catalogued as Add. 39843 by the British Library.

[82] Louvain Bibl. de l'Université G.53, ff. 186v-187v. This manuscript was a casualty of war.

[83] Chesney, 16.

perfectly clear that the same planning went into their production and that they emanated from the same workshop."[84]

The English manuscripts, for their part, follow the narrative structure of the earliest French manuscript, the Yates Thompson 11, while two later manuscripts, Harley 5272 and Jesus College, Cambridge, Q.D.4, omit the penultimate episode with the attacks by the four Daughters of Hell and instead segue into *The Charter of the Abbey of the Holy Ghost,* a conflation which marks them as later versions of the English treatises. The later English versions that precede the fifteenth-century construction of the Douce 365 *L'Abbaye du saint esprit* may have influenced the specific ending of that French redaction, created at the request of Margaret of York upon her marriage to Charles the Bold. This study will consider the possible audiences for, and influences on the earliest French treatises while analyzing the Douce 365 *L'Abbaye du saint esprit* with its additions and revisions that are devotional, spiritual, and political in nature.

---

[84] Ibid.

CHAPTER 2

CONSIDERATIONS OF GENDER
AND TEXT RECEPTION

From the mid-fourteenth to the late fifteenth century, the audience for *L'Abbaye du saint esprit* most likely included beguines, the institutionally religious, devout laypeople, the spiritually curious, and the socially mobile intent upon gaining a kind of spiritual recognition through ardent devotions. Of these audiences, Nicole Rice views the last two last groups as having sought a certain religious *caché* stemming from "spiritual ambition" which she defines as "a desire for the highest distinctions in the religious realm: assurance of salvation in the next life, and the possibility, in this life, of seeing and experiencing personal closeness to God through contemplation."[85] The participation in spiritual confraternities,[86] Rice explains, expanded a layperson's affiliation to such a religious order in spite of one's lack of formal religious vows. The lay devout in these confraternities could have been drawn to a work such as *L'Abbaye du saint esprit* through its statement of intended audience[87] and its specific focus on creating a metaphorical abbey of the heart. The text could well, of course, have also been appreciated by those who sought a more profound spiritual relationship with the Divine, un-influenced by "spiritual ambition" (in the sense of "upward striving") and who did not find a fulfilling spiritual relationship to be fully fostered at that time by the institutional Church. This view is supported by Christiana Whitehead who finds the individual emphasis of the English *Abbey of the Holy Ghost* to be "anti-monastic," noting that it coincides with "a crisis of fervor in coenobitic mo-

---

[85] Rice, 224.

[86] Groups which maintained special connections with religious orders through donations.

[87] Those persons who would like to be cloistered religious but could not be for various reasons.

nasticism" and with the desire of a "literate urban populace" for a more "personal religious experience."[88] Whatever an individual's reasons for pursuing spiritual knowledge, and there must have been many, devotional treatises became quite popular among both males and females in the fourteenth and fifteenth centuries, causing questions to arise in scholarship as to the initial audience for *L'Abbaye du saint esprit*. To gain greater clarity regarding the initial and early audiences for the French *L'Abbaye du saint esprit,* the present chapter will discuss questions related to audience and Victorine influence, allegory and gender, and the possible ownership of specific manuscripts themselves.

Audience and Victorine Influence

The earliest extant version of *L'Abbaye du saint esprit*, the Yates Thompson 11 manuscript and its associated, fragmented copy, Add 20697,[89] state only that the abbey is located "spiritually in the conscience": "La sainte abbaie et la religion doit estre fondee espirituellement en la conscience" (f.2, ll. 1-7). This early manuscript and its copy make no gendered reference to a particular audience nor do they specify that this redaction was written for those who would like to enter "into religion" but cannot (as do later French versions).[90] Because of this omission, this earliest redaction of *L'Abbaye du saint esprit* might not necessarily have been written for

---

[88] Whitehead, 16. Whitehead also notes that *The Abbey* includes support for the institutional Church, with the treatise's cleansing of the abbey from sin, the appointment of Shrift and Penance, and its mention of the ecclesiastical sacrament of Holy Communion in the description of Meditation's wheat (17). In the treatise, Whitehead notices that the religious of *The Abbey* must place their hope in "the uncontrollable operation of external grace" and thus demonstrate a "salutary mistrust in their own collective abilities exercised without recourse to the spiritual realm from which they draw their meaning" (18).

[89] The earliest two French manuscripts, Yates Thompson 11 and Add. 20697 (a fragment which follows the text of the Yates Thompson 11 closely, while omitting its miniatures), are similar, with the latter treatise following the former closely. They both present a relatively simple narrative core, with the Add. 20697 *L'Abbaye* ending three folios before the end of the Yates Thompson 11 treatise.

[90] Both the Royal 16.xii *L'Abbaye* of the late 14th century and the Douce 365 treatise of the mid-15th century contain this statement of intended audience. See Royal 16E.xii, f. 132, ll. 8-16 and Douce 365, f. 1, ll. 6-10.

those who had not taken institutional vows. Instead, it might well have been written for cloistered contemplatives attached to the Order of St. Victor, a religious order that emphasized spiritual renewal through contemplation and that often used architectural structures as mnemonics.[91] In such a context, the readers, male or female, of the earliest *L'Abbaye du saint esprit* could have found the spiritual lessons of the treatise enriched as they went about their daily routine, associating the various virtues and charitable works with the monastic architecture that surrounded them.

Such a confluence of immediate environment and textual reference coincides with the pedagogical thrust of Hugh of St. Victor's monastic reading model, encouraging the use of an abbatial metaphor for a cloistered audience. In this model, Hugh of St. Victor advocates the use of concrete forms to anchor religious abstractions and notes that "…there are two things that restore the divine likeness in man, namely the contemplation of truth and the practice of virtue."[92] In order to approach divine Wisdom, man is to consider the "finite or defined," in this case scripture and a concrete abstraction such as an abbey, and then proceed through the use of allegory and morality to knowledge of the "infinite or undefined," – here, religious principles of behavior.[93] Not only does this process allow for easier comprehension of spiritual abstractions but it also serves to enhance

---

[91] In the mid-twelfth century, Hugh of Fouilloy wrote *De Claustro animae*, a work built on the allegory of a metaphorical cloister which represented the contemplative soul. Similar to *L'Abbey du saint esprit,* this work paired various mental attributes with areas of the cloister: Reason with the chapter house, consideration of scripture with the refectory, tranquility with the dormitory. The abstractions in *De Claustro animae* often differed from those in *L'Abbaye* in being states of mind rather than specifically spiritual attributes; yet, the allegorical use of monastic architecture was similar enough to cause confusion when it came to authorial attribution of the later *L'Abbaye du saint esprit.* So strong is the correlation between *L'Abbaye,* the Victorine School, and the pedagogy of the *Didascalicon* that early attributions credited Hugh of St. Victor with authorship of *L'Abbaye du saint esprit* despite the absence of a Latin original, an ascription that has since fallen into disfavor largely because of manuscript dating. (See Whitehead, 3-6, 14.) C. Horstmann mentions a Latin original entitled *Abbacia de S. Spiritu* which he noted was lost. (C. Horstmann, 321.) Three French manuscripts from the third redaction of the text attribute *L'Abbaye du saint esprit* to Hugh of St. Victor: Bruxelles Bibl. Roy. 9555-58, B.L. Add. Ms. 29986, and B.N.F. Nouv.Acq. Fr. 5232; the treatise is also attributed to Jean Gerson at the beginning of the Douce 365 treatise.

[92] Hugh of St. Victor, *The Didascalicon,* I.54-55.

[93] Hugh of St. Victor, III. 92.

memory, clearly a key consideration in the structural design of *L'Abbaye du saint esprit*.[94] The foundation for such learning, then, lies in the "history" (designated as "scripture") from which allegory and morality proceed: "You have in history the means through which to admire God's deeds, in allegory the means through which to believe his mysteries, in morality the means through which to imitate his perfection."[95] In *L'Abbaye,* we see references to this "history" not only in the use of scripture to support the various *dicta* but also in the citations from Old Testament prophets, the apostles, and Church fathers found throughout the third and fourth redactions of the treatise. Further, the foundation for the abbey is laid stone-by-stone using "*vraye foy*"[96] in apparent imitation of Hugh of St. Victor's suggestion in the *Didascalicon* to measure the foundation using the "taut cord [that] shows the path of true faith."[97] This faith provides the "foundation of unshakable truth upon which the entire superstructure may rest…"[98] so that the ensuing exposition, including "the letter, the sense, and the deeper meaning (*sententia*),"[99] may be constructed securely in the Truth.[100]

The strength of the Victorine tradition and its influence on *L'Abbaye du saint esprit*, together with the lack of a specified gender for the audience are particularly notable in the case of the Yates Thompson 11 manuscript. This particular treatise is of a very high quality, written in a near-perfect scribal hand, with three elegant miniatures, including the full-page, elaborate illustration of aristocratic women (most likely the allegorical *figurae* of the treatise) processing to Mass, as discussed in Chapter 1.[101] The Yates Thompson 11 treatise, dating to c.1300, represents the earliest extant French manuscript of *L'Abbaye*;"[102] yet, it seems

---

[94] As cloistered readers meditatively walked through an abbey, the architecture would call to mind particular virtues and charitable acts from the treatise.

[95] Hugh of St. Victor, VI.138.

[96] "True faith," Douce 365, f. 2v, l. 15.

[97] Hugh of St. Victor, VI, 142.

[98] Hugh of St. Victor, VI.144.

[99] Hugh of St. Victor VI.147.

[100] Deborah McGrady offers an overview of the importance of the Hugh of St. Victor's *Didascalicon* on late medieval reading models in *Controlling Readers: Guillaume de Machaut and His Late Medieval Audience* (Buffalo: U of Toronto P, 2006), 25-32.

[101] See front cover of this book.

[102] *Catalogue of Additions to the Manuscripts in the British Museum*, 1854-1860, 211.

unlikely a first redaction would arrive from the mind so fully and beautifully "birthed." To this researcher, the superb state of the Yates Thompson 11 argues for the existence of an earlier, lost version of the French *L'Abbaye* or for a lost Latin original.[103] If this be the case, an early *L'Abbaye du saint esprit* could well have been written for contemplatives attached to the Order of St. Victor.

The argument for an early audience comprised of male and female lay devout rests most securely on a statement found at the beginning of the fourteenth-century Royal 16E.XII manuscript of Chesney's third redaction of the treatise:

> Many people would like to enter into religion but cannot because of poverty, ties of marriage, or another reason. For these people is made a book so that those (m. and f.) who cannot not enter into religion temporally may enter into religion spiritually. (f. 132, ll. 8-21)[104]

The Royal 16E.XII represents the earliest extant treatise to indicate that *L'Abbaye du saint esprit* was written for both males and females as indicated by its inclusion of both male and female demonstrative pronouns (*cil ou celles*) when describing the target audience: those who wish to be professed religious but cannot be for various reasons. This redaction was also created approximately a hundred years after the Yates Thompson 11 treatise.[105]

A similar statement of audience can also be found early in the fifteenth-century Douce 365 *L'Abbaye* of the fourth redaction of the treatise, dated to 1468:

> Many people would like very much to be "in religion" but they cannot because of poverty, or because they are held by ties of marriage, or for another reason. For these people, a 'religion' of

---

[103] At least one researcher, Janice Pinder of Monash University, feels the dates of the early manuscripts could be revised (private email, 2003).

[104] Mout de gent voudroient entrer en religion et ne puent ou pour pourete ou pour ce que il sont retenu par lian de mariage ou pour aucune reson. Pour si fes un livre que cil ou celles qui ne puent entrer en religion temporale soient en religion espirituele (Royal 16E.XII, f. 132, ll. 8-21).

[105] In the quotes above, the Royal 16E.XII treatise contains the demonstrative pronouns "cil" (m.) and "celles" (f.) in the quote above, while the Douce 365 contains "ceulz" (m.) and "celles" (f.).

the abbey of the Holy Spirit is made in the heart, so that all those who cannot be 'in religion' physically might be able to be 'in religion' spiritually. (f. 1, ll. 6-13)[106]

The Douce 365 *L'Abbaye du saint esprit* was created approximately two hundred years after the earliest extant version of *L'Abbaye du saint esprit* found in the Yates Thompson 11 (dated to c.1300) which states only that the abbey is located spiritually in the conscience. Therefore, the Royal 16E.XII and Douce 365 treatises do not represent a reliable identification of the treatise's initial audience,[107] but do reflect a growing interest in the treatise among a lay audience.

More pointedly, the fourteenth-century Royal 16E.XII treatise also includes a reference to textile work in a passage on meditation in which "…spiritual people in prayer" [become so entranced that] "the spindle has fallen to one side and the distaff to the other," [as they swoon] "just as the lark swoons in singing" (Royal 16E.XII, ff. 135, ll. 33-34; 135v, ll. 51-53; 135v, ll. 55-56).[108] Based on the textile occupation of many beguines, this quote has been used to argue solely for a beguine audience for the Royal 16E.XII treatise; however, this assumption ignores the identification of a male and female audience as indicated by plural demonstrative pronouns in the manuscript's initial statement of audience quoted above.

---

[106] "…[M]out de gens voldroient bien estre en religion maiz ilz ne peuent ou par pourete ou par ce quilz sont par loyen de marriage retenue ou par aultre raison. C'est pour tant fay une religion en ton coeur del abbaye du saint esperit pourquoy tous ceulz et celles [m. & f.] qui estre ne peuent en religion corporelle puissent estre en religion espirituelle" (Douce 365, f. 1, ll.6-13).

[107] Add. Ms. 29986 (c. 14th century) of the second redaction is the first extant manuscript to include a statement of audience, stating that the abbey is located in "la consaence domme (of man) et de femme (of woman)" (f. 149v, l. 41). The statement of audience contained in the Royal 16E.XII and Douce 365 treatises has been used to argue solely for an early, if not initial, audience of beguines; this view proves to be erroneous for the reasons stated above.

[108] "genz esperitueus après oroison" become so entranced that "…li fuisiaus leur cheoit dune part et la quenoille dautre" as they swoon "comme l'aloese pasme en chantant" (Royal 16E. XII, ff. 135, ll. 33-34; 135v, ll. 51-53; 135v, ll. 55-56).

"Fille" and the Ungendered Soul

The early French manuscripts of the first redaction, Yates Thompson 11 and Add. 20697, do contain a single direct address of *Fille* (Daughter), used when admonishing the reader in the guarding of the senses: "Daughter [*Fille*], if you wish to be truly religious, guard your enclosure: close your heart from evil thoughts, your eyes from foolish looking, your ears from hearing evil words, your mouth from laughing lightly and from foolishly speaking."[109] This apparent address of a female religious may appear to make a case for a single female reader, as in the opinion of N.F. Blake;[110] however, the address of *Fille* here may just as well constitute an address of the individual Christian soul, as noted in another context by Constant Mews of Monash University.[111] The perfect soul was, as Mews notes, "understood as a supremely beautiful woman who leaves her father's house for her spiritual beloved."[112] *"Fille,"* as the redeemed soul, recalls the Beloved of the *Song of Songs* and the admonition found in Psalm 44:11-12 of the Vulgate bible: "Listen, daughter, and see, and incline your ear, and forget your people and your father's house, and the king shall greatly desire thy beauty."[113] To the cloistered religious, male or female, this verse calls the individual soul to forget one's family and the secular world and to cleave to God as experienced in the conventual life.

The designation of *Fille* to represent the perfect Soul marks an especially effective way to introduce the passage on enclosure in *L'Abbaye du saint esprit*. As Caroline Walker Bynum has made clear, feminized religious language referring to the souls of both male and female religious permeates medieval spirituality.[114] As Bynum notes, there are several forces that encourage this feminization of the

---

[109] "Fille, veuz ester bien religieuse, tien te close. Gard ton cloistre. Clo ton cuer de mauvaisement penser, tes eulz de folement regarder, tes oreiller de males paroles escouter, ta bouche de rire legierment et de folement parller." (Yates Thompson 11, f. 2v, ll. 31-39). See also Add. 20697, f. 29v, ll. 9-16.

[110] N.F. Blake, 89.

[111] See Constant Mews, "Introduction," *Listen, Daughter* (New York: Palgrave, 2001) 1-2.

[112] Mews, 1.

[113] Ibid. "Audi filia et vide et inclina aurem tuam et obliviscere populum tuum et domun patris tui et concupiscet rex decorum tuum."

[114] Carolyn Walker Bynum, 135-146.

soul.[115] First, the gender of *anima* (soul) is feminine in Latin grammar. Next, during the twelfth-century, an increasing identification of the individual Soul with the Bride of the *Song of Songs* develops in scriptural exegesis. In addition, the weakness then often associated with women was used in a religious context to connote positively the humility of the obedient soul; and, finally, there was a growing tendency to associate "female erotic and sexual experience" with "the soul's union with Christ."[116]

In *L'Abbaye du saint esprit, "Fille"* resonates not only with the "daughter" of Psalm 44 but also with the Beloved of the *Song of Songs,* and contains a nuanced tone of implied subordination and affectivity. Speaking of the *Speculum Virginum* which also makes use of the phrase "Listen, Daughter," Constant Mews has noted, there is a "profound ambiguity in the phrase 'Listen, daughter'...: ...At one level, it is the voice of authority enjoining obedience and submission. At another, it is a call to step out of what is familiar and to use one's senses to imagine oneself as a bride who must prepare herself to meet her beloved."[117] This injunction, as Constance Mews points out, had a "particular resonance for women who sought to dedicate themselves to the religious life,"[118] robed as it was in a scriptural authority that challenges the reader with spiritual dedication and the promise of adventure. *"Fille,"* in introducing the passage on spiritual containment in *L'Abbaye du saint esprit,* directs and reinforces the admonition to guard the senses and, by extension, the soul, against worldly assault. The warning itself implies the guidance of a superior or spiritual advisor, while the direct address, *"Fille"* serves rhetorically to underscore the significance of this passage on containment.

The address *"Fille"* has led to an early consideration of beguines as a possible initial audience for *L'Abbbaye du saint esprit,* as those who might have wished to enhance devotions that were, by the nature of their sisterhood, practiced outside of a specific religious order. *"Fille,"* however, can also refer to the redeemed, spiritually-feminized soul of either gender.

---

[115] The following three points are from Bynum, *ibid.*

[116] Bynum 138. In Bernard's Sermon 12, par. 8, Bernard "calls himself a woman [to indicate]... his weakness and ...need for contemplation," qtd. in Bynum, *Jesus as Mother*, n. 63, p.128.

[117] Mews, 11.

[118] Mews, 1.

Female Allegory and Audience

As noted above, early scholarly discussion of *L'Abbaye du saint esprit* has often assumed that the work was written solely for a female audience. The presence of female allegorical figures in the text led Hope Emily Allen to find the work "originally written for women…and perhaps…for lay women of high position," with an eye to "comfort[ing] the worldly with assurance of the holiness possible in lay estate."[119] In 1972, N.F. Blake noted that the "French texts [of *L'Abbaye du saint esprit*] are addressed to a 'sister' only,"[120] although it now appears that the use of *Fille* (Daughter) does not necessarily constitute an unambiguous indication of the treatise's initial audience and is not borne out textually in later French redactions of the earliest texts. Consequently, the two earliest French manuscripts[121] contain few unambiguous clues regarding the gender of the initial audience even though the abbey is peopled by female personifications of spiritual virtues and charitable acts. These abstractions, however, do not give us concrete surety of an initial female reception of the text as an abbey would be an appropriate locus for the feminized soul of Psalm 44 (whether embodied as male or female) or the Beloved of the *Song of Songs,* to inhabit. Further, the second and later redactions of *L'Abbaye du saint esprit* of the treatise address both male and female audiences while still addressing the soul as *Fille*.

The precedent of the classical tradition in setting the standard for the presentation of allegorical *figurae* also contributes to their feminization. In this tradition, as Maureen Quilligan has pointed out, the abstractions are allegorized as female because the grammatical rules of Latin have made them so. In discussing Boethius' Lady Philosophy in *The Consolation of Philosophy*, Quilligan notes that

> [t]he gender of this conventional scene is due essentially to the exigencies of grammar: personifications of abstractions such as Philosophy and Nature take the feminine form primarily because

---

[119] H. E. Allen, 337.

[120] N.F. Blake, n. 3, p. 89. Blake also suggests, "…the work may originally have been written for a woman since the abbey is staffed with nuns" (89).

[121] The Yates Thompson 11 and Add. 20697.

allegory always works narratively by literalizing lexical effects. The gender of abstract nouns made from verbs in Latin is always feminine – *auctoritas* itself, for instance, is feminine – so the personifications embodying these concepts take on the gender of the words....[122]

For *L'Abbaye du saint esprit*, the abstractions of spiritual virtues (Humility, Mercy, Patience, Wisdom, Faith, to name a few) and spiritual acts (Charity, Prayer, Meditation, among others) are also feminized, following the process Quilligan identifies in various medieval texts, including Dante's *The Divine Comedy*.[123] As Joan Ferrante has also noted, allegorical abstractions are increasingly portrayed as female in twelfth-century writing.[124] Latin grammar, the use of an allegorical abbey to represent the individual Christian's conscience, and classical precedent can all explain the female allegorical virtues of *L'Abbaye du saint esprit*.

We have seen that the second (Add. 29986), third (16E.XII), and fourth (Douce 365) redactions all address both males and females. As to be expected, the mid-fourteenth-century English versions[125] of the treatise that participated in the popular movement of English lay spirituality included both genders as members of their audiences, as well. Although the gender of the intended audience for *L'Abbaye* may appear ambiguous in the earliest redaction of the treatise containing the Yates Thompson 11 and the Add. 20697 manuscripts, the remaining French manuscripts of the fourteenth century refer specifically to both male and female readers.

Early Ownership of the French Manuscripts

The first French manuscripts, the elegantly illustrated Yates Thompson 11 of c. 1300 of and its incomplete copy the Add. 20697 were created at the time

[122] Maureen Quilligan, *The Allegory of Female Authority* (Ithaca: Cornell U P, 1991), 23-25.
[123] Quilligan, 18-31.
[124] Joan Ferrante in Bynum, 138.
[125] See Bibliography for a list of Middle English manuscripts containing *The Abbey of the Holy Ghost*.

when beguine communities were forming in the Low Countries; however, Walter Simons notes that beguine communities sprang up "more or less simultaneously, without central coordination, and…without a single point of origin or a single founder."[126] Simons points out that the early organization of the movement was diffuse, that many beguines participated for a time and then entered convents, and that the movement resisted "strict enclosure."[127] Under these circumstances, it seems difficult to believe that the Yates Thompson 11 treatise of the first redaction, with its three finely-detailed, full-page miniatures, and its beautifully executed script would have been created for the more humble beguines, although it is clearly not impossible given the lack of a specified gender in the text. Instead, it appears that this manuscript was commissioned by an aristocrat of some wealth,[128] an assertion reinforced by Chesney's finding that it later belonged to Jean, Duke de Berry, and subsequently to his niece, Marie de Bourbon.[129]

The remaining redactions of the French *L'Abbaye du saint esprit* all indicate that they are written to be read by both males and females, whether so indicated by the use of male and female demonstrative pronouns or by a clear statement of audience, as in the case with the second redaction that contains the French Add. 29986, a manuscript said to have belong to "John, Duke of Berry, son of John, King of France."[130] In the later third and fourth redactions, the language becomes more formal and courtly, as seen in the Royal 16E.XII *L'Abbaye* which appealed to an aristocratic audience. This manuscript also bears the initial "H.R.," thereby indicating a possible royal ownership at some point by Henry VII or Henry VIII, according to the *Catalogue of Western Manuscripts in the Old Royal* (198). With its lavish illuminations and formal metaphors, this treatise cannot reasonably be considered one of the earliest versions of *L'Abbaye du saint esprit* or be created for the more humble beguines.

---

[126] Walter Simons, *Cities of Ladies: Beguine Communities in the Medieval Low Countries, 1200-1565* (Philadelphia: U of Penn P, 2003), 48. See Simons, 36-48.

[127] Simons, 44-48.

[128] Paul Meyer described the Yates Thompson 11 as "un très beau livre, richement orné." (53).

[129] Chesney, 14.

[130] *Catalogue of Additions to the Manuscripts of the British Library, 1876-1881* (London: Trustees of the British Museum, 1967), 16. One treatise in this manuscript, *Le Livre de mirour des dames"* was said to be dedicated to "Jeanne, Queen of France and Navarre (the wife of Philippe le Bel)," (15).

Following the first redaction of the treatise, *L'Abbaye du saint esprit* was consciously written for a courtly audience of both genders, at the same time that the redactions continued the use of *"Fille"* to represent the redeemed soul of the individual reader. It seems likely, because of provenance, exquisite workmanship, and later ownership by Jean Duke de Berry of the Yates Thompson 11 treatise, that the *L'Abbaye du saint esprit* of the first redaction was also written for a courtly audience, rather than for beguines.

Spindles, Books, and Gender

Finally, the argument that textile production provides proof of an original Beguine audience cannot be maintained. First, the passage which prompts this view from researchers is taken from the Royal 16E.XII *L'Abbaye,* a fourteenth-century manuscript that is clearly courtly in tone, contains elevated language and additional material, includes a passage on good governance, and addresses both sexes as its intended audience. The passage, in which the quotation is found, discusses prayer, noting St. Gregory's mention of a "…very great joy that is aroused in the soul by grace after prayer" which sometimes causes "spiritual people after prayer" to be so carried away that they cannot keep from singing and swooning.[131] At these times, according to the passage, "It can so happen that each is so carried away where they sit that the spindle may fall to one side and the distaff to another, the book or the psalter, and they swoon as the lark swoons in singing."[132]

The mention of the spindle and distaff in this metaphor concerning affective prayer is found only in the Royal 16E.XII *L'Abbaye du saint esprit* and has been taken to prove that the intended audience was comprised of (female) beguines.

---

[131] "…tres gr[a]nt joie qui est meue en lame par grace après oroison," … "genz esperitueus après oroison" (Royal 16E.XII, f. 135, ll. 25-28 and ll. 33-34).

[132] …si puet bien estre auenue que aucunes ont este si rauies la ou eles se seoient que lifeuisiaus leur cheoit dune part et la quenoille dautre li liure u sautier et cheoient pasme es ausi comme laloese pasme en chanta[n]t" (ff. 135, l. 46 -135v, l. 6). It is noteworthy that a parallel passage in the later Douce 365 *L'Abbaye*, that is derived from the Royal 16E.XII version and also written for a noble audience, ends with tapping toes and happiness, omitting the reference to the spindle, distaff, book and psalter falling and to the swooning, as singing larks, of the people praying.

In mentioning spinners to illustrate how some spiritual people respond affectively to prayer, the treatise most probably refers to a metaphor in Sermon 12 of Bernard of Clairvaux in which the saint "compares monks to women who remain at home spinning while their husbands, i.e. bishops, go out to war."[133] Bynum notes that Bernard uses "sexually inverted images" in which men are referred to as women as a way of expressing "personal dependence and the dependence of one's values on God."[134] In this context, the monks wait with humility, meditating as they actively pray and worship God. The rapturous experience suggested by the passage in *L'Abbaye du saint esprit* could have occurred to monks in contemplation as well as to nuns, as Bernard of Clairvaux's metaphor suggests, so that this passage alone cannot be claimed for one gender at the exclusion of the other and certainly not to one religious group, such as the beguines. This reference to Bernard's writings is one of many to be found in *L'Abbaye du saint esprit*, and is here found in a manuscript that acknowledges both a male and female audience.[135]

This passage also includes the possession of a book or psalter by the person praying, in addition to the mention of the spindle and distaff. Deborah McGrady notes that in the thirteenth century, illustrators of devotional texts began replacing with a book, the spindle often held by the Virgin Mary in annunciation scenes, a change which emphasized Mary's association with the Messianic prophesies of the Old Testament and her relationship to Christ as the Word made flesh expressed in the first chapter of the gospel of John.[136] McGrady theorizes that "[w]here Mary could approach God on the sinner's behalf, the book could serve as a gateway to enlightenment."[137] Thus, artists in portraying Mary with a book emphasized her role as mother of Christ, the Word, and as intercessor

---

[133] Bynum, n. 63, p. 128. For a discussion of women's use of inverted imagery, Bynum cites Jo Ann McNamara, "Sexual Equality and the Cult of Virginity in Early Christian Thought," *Feminist Studies* 3.3/4 (1976): 145-158. In Bernard's "Sermon 12," see particularly paragraphs 8 and 9.

[134] Bynum, 128.

[135] The passage itself suggests a male and female audience as books and psalters would traditionally be associated with males, as spinning might be with females.

[136] McGrady, Deborah, *Controlling Readers: Guillaume de Machaut and His Late Medieval Audience* (Buffalo: U of Toronto P, 2006), 32.

[137] Ibid.

between God and humanity, while simultaneously emphasizing the book as a helpful aid to the transformative spiritual experience. Similarly, *L'Abbaye du saint esprit* seeks to help the devout reader build an abbey in the heart for meditational purposes. It stands to reason that here the images of the distaff, a tool of busyness, and the book, an aid to meditation, may well represent the balanced life of both the spiritually mature woman and man, while symbolizing the humility of the obedient soul, regardless of physical gender, and represent the devout's expectant hope for enlightenment during meditation. Further, the dropping of the distaff, spindle, book, or psalter might also indicate the leaving off of daily "busy-ness" in order to rest in meditative stillness and experience the Divine. The book itself as an aid to a transformative experience could also emphasize the authority of the treatise itself to lead the reader closer to God.

Finally, if this passage were meant to be taken literally, and in an allegorical text it seems plausible that it is not, this observation could apply to a great many people, not to beguines alone, given the ubiquitous nature of spinning and weaving in the Middle Ages. As is well known, during this time of largely subsistence living, the great majority of people were involved in an aspect of weaving as were their children who were often employed winding spindles, while cloistered nuns produced intricate textiles, especially altar cloths, chasubles and other items meant to enhance corporate worship.[138] Textile production, of course, was a continuous occupation that supported medieval society in most of its various manifestations and cannot be accurately considered the purview of beguines alone.

A Complexity in Manuscript Transmission

One cannot definitively state that *L'Abbaye du saint esprit* was originally written solely for a female audience, and there are good reasons for not rushing to embrace that assumption. This is not to say, however, that a beguine audience could never have comprised its readership at any point in the treatise's evolution. The Louvain Bibliothèque de l'Université G.53 manuscript, lost to war in 1944,

---

[138] For excellent examples and discussion of needlework completed by medieval nuns, see *Sur la Terre comme au ciel: Jardins d'Occident á la fin du Moyen Age.* Paris: Musées nationaux, 2002.

contained an abbreviated version of *L'Abbaye du saint esprit* between folios 186v and 187v. Chesney places the Louvain *L'Abbaye* within the third redaction of the treatise that contains the fourteenth-century Royal 16E.XII manuscript. Its location in Louvain, if indeed it were created nearby, and the confluence of the work's creation during a time when the beguine life was growing ever more popular, make the claim for a later fourteenth-century beguine readership quite plausible.[139] That does not indicate, however, that beguines constituted the targeted audience for the earliest version of *L'Abbaye du saint esprit* or that the original readership was necessarily exclusively female.

The content of *L'Abbaye du saint esprit* itself argues for a Victorine provenance with the two earliest manuscripts meant for a recipient, male or female, in a cloistered setting. The treatise in its early form certainly owes a debt of influence to the Victorine School established outside of Paris in the early twelfth century; for its part, the later, fifteenth-century Douce 365 treatise of the fourth redaction contains references to the principles of *devotio moderna* while continuing many Victorine characteristics. The Victorines, as Canons Regular, emphasized scholarship, exegesis, contemplation, and compassion while embracing the communal life, the mystery of Divinity, and the manifestation of the Spirit in all things.[140] These elements can be seen in the French and English versions of *L'Abbaye du saint esprit* with its use of the monastic teaching model; its encouragement of meditation, charitable acts, and monastic virtues; and its inclusion of specific scriptural and patristic references, including the treatise's embrace of Bernardian exegesis.

The later redactions of *L'Abbaye du saint esprit* which specify a readership that would have liked to have taken holy orders but could not for various reasons, clearly became popular with aristocrats of both genders, as the manuscript

---

[139] See Walter Simons, *Cities of Ladies: Beguine Communities in the Medieval Low Countries, 1200-1565* (Philadelphia: U of Penn P, 2001), 56-59. Simons notes the rapid growth of the Beguines in the Low Countries during this period.

[140] Stephen Chase, *Contemplation and Compassion: The Victorine Tradition* (Maryknoll: Orbis, 2003) 16. Chase give this "summary of the Victorine ideal: the spiritual and contemplative exploration of the inner person accomplished under the guidance, supervision, and love of the community intent on union with God through imitation of Christ in order to become an example to others" (25).

ownership attests.[141] Chesney also finds Add. 20697, the incomplete copy of the Yates Thompson *L'Abbaye* to have belonged to the Chaplain to Blanche, widow of Philip VI.[142] From these references and from the Douce 365 commissioning by Margaret of York as well as the Royal 16E.XII marginal initials of "H.R.," we know that the treatise quickly found favor with an aristocratic readership.[143] Further, the courtly language of these specific versions of the treatise testifies to their popularity among the nobility.

L'Abbaye du saint esprit, then, in its eleven extant French manuscripts, evolved from a relatively simple text that could have been written for a cloistered audience of males and females, according to textual evidence. The earliest two manuscripts do not specifically mentioned that the work is written for those who wish to be "in religion" but cannot be for various reasons; rather, they establish the abbey "spiritually in the conscience" of the reader. Without the parameter of denied access to religious orders, the provenance of the treatise opens up to encompass an audience that is cloistered, thereby making the allegorical abbey and its lessons more immediately relevant to its readers' daily lives. The treatise soon extends its appeal to an aristocratic audience and moves rather quickly to acknowledge openly a male and female readership. It could also have appealed to a beguine audience, particularly in its later forms, and in its English manifestations, it was popular as a vernacular text appropriate for lay devotions, as its presence in twenty-four extant English manuscripts attests.

Clearly, *L'Abbaye du saint esprit,* as a treatise, resists the oversimplification of its initial reception. A complex work not written solely for beguines, *L'Abbaye* moves within and adapts to various textual environments, reflecting the fluidity of late medieval manuscript transmission while testifying to the French and English textual reciprocity thriving during this period. It challenges us to acknowledge the many similarities among various late-medieval religious groups and underscores the difficulty of designating an original readership based on a

---

[141] See above.

[142] Chesney, 14.

[143] With the ownership of Add. 29986 by "John, Duke of Berry, son of John, King of France," it becomes clear that at least one manuscript from each of the four French redactions was owned by royalty. For the ownership of Add. 29986, see *Catalogue of Additions to the Manuscripts of the British Library, 1876-81,* 16.

shared occupation with textiles, contemplation, affective language, and religious allegory. In so doing, *L'Abbaye du saint esprit* reminds us of the complexity of early medieval textual environments and offers a more nuanced view of initial reception than that previously proposed for this treatise.

CHAPTER 3

THE DOUCE 365 *L'ABBAYE DU SAINT ESPRIT* AND ITS BURGUNDIAN CONTEXT

The French Yates Thompson 11 *L'Abbaye du saint esprit* dates from c. 1300, some fifty-eight years before the earliest extant English version of the text.[144] Based on this manuscript dating, then, the treatise originated in France and moved from that country to England relatively soon afterward. The various English redactions of *The Abbey of the Holy Ghost*, notable for their similarity of content within the English tradition, contain certain additions and omissions in relation to the French treatises. Each English treatise contains mystical material, and all but two of them follow the narrative framework of the earliest French manuscript, Yates Thompson 11.[145] The mysticism of the English treatises may well have influenced that of the later French Royal 16E.xii *L'Abbaye* which appears to have resulted from a meditative reworking of an earlier redaction. The Royal 16E.xii, having belonged to a King Henry, as mentioned earlier, may well have been known to Margaret of York,[146] sister to Edward IV and Richard III

---

[144] This English redaction is located in Ms. Winchester College 33. The date is noted by D. Peter Consacro according to *The Catalogue* Librorum Manuscriptorum, 1697, in *A Critical Edition of the Abbey of the Holy Ghost from All Known Extant English Manuscripts with Introduction, Notes, and Glossary. Diss. Fordham, 1971.*

[145] The two variant manuscripts, Harley 5272 and Jesus College, Cambridge, Q.D.4, omit the episode concerning the four daughters of hell and segue into *The Charter of the Abbey of the Holy Ghost*, a work of a completely different nature than *The Abbey.* (See Chapter 2.)

[146] Nigel Morgan suggests that Margaret's mother, the devout Cecily Neville, may have influenced Margaret's choice of devotional reading material: "Margaret's choice of reading matter could have been determined in England, perhaps under the influence of her pious mother, Cicely. The inclusion of works popular in England, such as *The Abbey of the Holy Ghost*, Grosseteste's *Chateau d'amour*,...and the extract of the life of the English Saint Edmund

of England. This popular work, in turn, may have influenced Margaret of York who commissioned the French *L'Abbaye du saint esprit* located in the Douce 365 manuscript upon her marriage to the Duke of Burgundy in 1468.

This commissioning of the Douce 365 *L'Abbaye* is significant as it derives from the Royal 16E.xii treatise, yet contains significant additions in the form of a 352-line dialogue between Christ and *Fille* ("Daughter" or the "Soul"), as well as additional direct addresses of *Fille* placed at key points within the text. The unique dialogue and direct addresses of *Fille* underscore tenets of *Devotio Moderna* of which Margaret was a *dévotée*, and emphasize Christian virtues which may have been perceived to be lacking, if not in Margaret, then in her husband, Charles the Bold, as he struggled to create a Lothringian middle state between Germany and France. In addition to the virtues delineated in the Douce 365 treatise, the work reminds Margaret, and ostensibly Charles, to beware of the dangers of arrogance and wealth, and to respect the divinity of kings at a time when Burgundy is embroiled in a war with the king of France. To provide a context for understanding the additions of the Douce 365 *L'Abbaye du saint esprit* analyzed in Chapter 4, this chapter will consider the manuscript's Burgundian context through representative actions of Charles the Bold and Margaret of York; discuss the duties of *écrivains*[147] and influences on the manuscript's scribe, David Aubert; and explicate *Devotio Moderna* as the devotional *milieu* in which the Douce 365 *L'Abbaye* is situated.

On June 14, 1468, Margaret of York departed from London aboard the *New Ellen* bound for Flanders and her forthcoming marriage to Charles the Bold, Duke of Burgundy. Behind this marriage lay economic and political concerns that were rooted in the turmoil of the Hundred Years' War between France and England that ended in 1453, and the Wars of the Roses still underway in England. During this period, English merchants amassed wealth in providing wool for export, particularly to Burgundy where merchants oversaw the creation of textiles that were subsequently imported into England for sale. Previously, according to M.-R.

---

appended to her *Apocalypse*, all provide some evidence that she [Cicely] may have played a part in the choice of her [Margaret's] texts" (70). Nigel Morgan, "Texts of Devotion and Religious Instruction Associated with Margaret of York," *Margaret of York, Simon Marmion, and The Visions of Tondal.* Ed. Thomas Kren. Malibu: J. Paul Getty Museum. 1992.

[147] Literally, "writers;" in this case, formally trained "scribes."

Theilemans, Chef de Travaux aux Archives Généraux du Royaume de Belgique, England had enriched her coffers at the expense of the Netherlands by an unequal trade exchange of silver and gold, and had banned the importation of Burgundian merchandise in England.[148] The Duke of Burgundy responded to this imbalance with a prohibition against English cloth. The marriage of Margaret of York and Charles the Bold sought to restore a balance in trade, and in 1469, a treaty between the two countries assured more financial parity in the market place.

In addition to the economic and political instability surrounding these conflicts, there existed Charles the Bold's determination to connect his scattered lands into one powerful state and to be crowned Vicar of the Empire or King of the Romans.[149] With his marriage to Margaret of York, Charles the Bold sought to renew an Anglo-Burgundian alliance that might thwart the ambitions of Louis XI of France who hoped to expand his kingdom to include lands under Burgundian control. In addition, because both Edward IV of England and Charles the Bold relied heavily upon loans from wool merchants in order to finance their military campaigns, they attached great importance to the upcoming Anglo-Burgundian marriage alliance[150] which would affect the economic and political ambitions of both countries.

Predictably, Louis XI, recognizing the benefits inherent in an Anglo-French alliance, sought to disrupt the wedding negotiations by proposing four possible candidates for Margaret's hand, one of which was Philip, Count of Bresse (Louis XI's brother-in-law).[151] At a conference near Rouen in 1467, the French king of-

---

[148] Theilemans, M.R. "Introduction," *Marguerite d'York et son temps.* (Brussels: Banque de Bruxelles, 1967) 7-8.

[149] Weightman Christine, *Margaret of York: Duchess of Burgundy 1446-1503* (New York: St. Martin's, 1989), 87. See Weightman for a discussion of the historical events surrounding Margaret of York's life. For other discussions of Margaret's political influence, see Wims Blockmans, "The Devotion of a Lonely Duchess." *Margaret of York, Simon Marmion, and The Visions of Tondal,* ed. Thomas Kren (Malibu: Getty, 1992) 29-46. For a discussion of the economic dispute specific to the wool trade, see M.R. Theilemans, "Introduction," 7-8, and Weightman 34-37.

[150] Weightman, 34.

[151] Weightman, 35. Weightman notes: "[Louis] could not find a candidate equal in status to Charles but he had assembled no less than four possible candidates: his brother-in-law Philip, Count of Bresse; René, Count of Alençon...; Philbert of Savoy, the young Prince of Piedmont; and Galeazzo Sforza, the new Duke of Milan..." (35).

fered to provide the bride's dowry, pay all costs of the wedding, give Edward IV a substantial pension, give trade concessions to English merchants, and consider a treaty dealing with economic and political concerns.[152] When Louis' offers were rejected, he persevered in his efforts by seeking to obstruct dowry loans, by trying to block the necessary papal dispensation, and by spreading unfounded rumors concerning Margaret's chastity.[153]

Against this backdrop of political intrigue, Margaret of York entered into a marriage with the Duke of Burgundy that strengthened Charles the Bold's position politically, at least in the short term. The marriage began with a lavish display of Burgundian wealth amid newsworthy festivities[154] and became the impetus for the creation of the Bodleian Library Douce 365 manuscript commissioned by Margaret of York. With this union, the personally devout Margaret would undertake the religious education of Charles's eleven-year-old daughter, Mary, a duty that Margaret took seriously as evidenced by her generous actions on behalf of the convents and by the closeness the two women shared later, after the untimely death of the child's father. This duty would include the inculcation of Christian virtues, a task that would be significantly supported by reading the spiritual advice of the allegorical figures in the Douce 365 *L'Abbaye du saint esprit.*

The Douce 365 manuscript contains several devotional works as well as a lengthy version of *L'Abbaye du saint esprit* addressed to both males and females that encourages spiritual formation in those who "want very much to be in religion but cannot…."[155] The Douce 365 treatise also contains significant additions over previous French versions of the text that, when viewed within their political and social context, render clear the intention of this redaction's scribe, David Aubert, to impart not only a spiritual message to the influential duchess but a political one as well.

---

[152] Weightman, 37.

[153] Weightman, 44.

[154] For information on the marriage of Charles the Bold and Margaret of York, see Weightman, 30-60; Richard Vaughan, *Charles the Bold: The Last Valois Duke of Burgundy.* (New York: Boydell, 2002), 48-53; Richard Barber, *The Pastons: A Family in the Wars of the Roses* (Woodbridge: Boydell, 1986), 140-1.

[155] Douce 365, f. 1, ll. 6-13. "…[Moult] de gens voudroient bien ester en religion maiz ils ne peuent…."

Charles the Bold's Style of Governance

At the time of his accession as Duke of Burgundy, Charles the Bold[156] was forced to contend with a great deal of turmoil in his territories, not only that precipitated by his claim to the duchy of Burgundy but also that left festering by his father, Philip the Good. Although closely related to the kings of France through his great-grandfather, Philip the Bold, brother of Charles V, Charles the Bold found himself in direct competition with French territorial and economic interests, as had earlier dukes of Burgundy. Upon his accession, Charles inherited vast land holdings, some of which were dependencies of the French, such as Flanders, while others, such as Liège, belonged to the Church and were therefore part of the Holy Roman Empire.[157] Despite conflicting and ecclesiastical claims, Charles could and did initiate several aggressive reforms within these lands in an effort to consolidate his power, a process he did not hesitate to set in motion. These reforms included tripling the amount of the *aides*[158] collected from the citizens, an action that allowed the duke to amass within one decade the total revenues that Philip the Good gathered in forty-five years.[159] Charles' reforms also included placing his own arbitrators trained in Roman law to judge the Flemish outside of their customary legal system, setting up his own *parlement*, reorganizing the Burgundian Church to move it closer toward being a state institution, and setting unpopular taxes on all church lands and property granted within the sixty years previous to 1474.[160] He often judged petitions himself publicly in front

---

[156] The currently-used French title *Charles le Téméraire* translates, in English, more accurately to Charles the Reckless or Charles the Rash. During his lifetime, he was often referred to as *Charles le Terrible,* a name given because of his cruelty and hot temper.

[157] See Vaughan, Chapter 1, p. 11ff, for information on Liège and the ecclesiastical principality of which it was the capital. I am indebted to Vaughan's study for much of this information on Charles the Bold's temperament and subjugation of Ghent, Liège, and Dinant.

[158] Taxes were used not only to assist the governed area but to pay costs for maintaining Charles' court and to support his numerous wars. Consequently, it is not surprising that Gunn finds "Charles' average annual expenditure [to be] more than twice that of his father" (28). Steven Gunn, "Henry VII and Charles the Bold: Brothers under the Skin?" *History Today* 46.4 (1996) 28. I am indebted to Gunn for his discussion of Charles the Bold's fiscal and judicial reforms.

[159] Gunn, 28.

[160] Gunn, 30. For a discussion of Charles the Bold's specific reforms, see Gunn, 28-30.

of nobles required to attend in order to emphasize his control, and also required his subjects to address him no longer as "most dread lord" but as "most dread and sovereign lord,"[161] an epithet which would recall his royal lineage and might validate his royal status if and when his various land holdings became unified. It is not surprising, then, that in 1475 a Milanese ambassador commented that "all [Charles'] thoughts… are about the acquisition for himself of immortal glory."[162]

At the time of his accession, Charles the Bold encountered the resistance of several powerful mercantile communities, the most persistent of which involved Ghent (the city in which David Aubert, the Douce 365 scribe, lived) and Liège;[163] to this dissent, Charles responded with the brutal savagery which became characteristic of his heavy-handed governance. As Richard Vaughan has described, the resistance in these two cities was exacerbated by civil disturbances between radical elements supported by the common people and civic leaders drawn from the powerful merchant class.[164] These disturbances provoked a riot against the local tax on June 28, 1467, during the festivities for St. Livinus, a day that marked the formal entry of Charles the Bold into Ghent as its newly crowned duke. Charles, striking an agitator in anger, exacerbated the situation, which escalated as the populace demanded that the gates of the city be reopened, that the use of guild banners be restored, that corrupt city officials be punished, that the power of the city's ruling class be curbed, and that the harsh settlement of 1453 which had quelled an earlier rebellion in Ghent be repealed.[165] Three days later, Charles managed to escape from Ghent with his daughter, Mary, and the treasure he brought from Bruges by promising concessions[166] which he later withdrew in a blunt, decisive, and authoritative manner.

By January of 1469, Charles dealt with the crisis at Ghent in a fashion

---

[161] Ibid.

[162] Gunn, 27.

[163] In light of his manuscript additions addressed to *"Fille"* (Daughter, Soul) in the Douce 365 *L'Abbaye*, it is significant that David Aubert, the scribe for the Douce 365 *L'Abbaye du saint esprit,* lived in Ghent. See Chapter 4, below.

[164] Vaughan, 5-6. For Vaughan's study of these conflicts in Ghent and Liège, see pp. 5-40. See also G. Chastellain, *Oeuvres.* Ed. Kervyn de Littenhove. *Académie royale de Belgique,* V. 249-78.

[165] Vaughan, 6.

[166] Ibid.

presumably much more to his liking. Calling a convocation in the great hall of Brussels[167] (attended by nobles from Liège, Looz, Savoy, Clèves, and Ravenstein, as well as the members of the Order of the Golden Fleece, ambassadors from other European countries, and the Queen of France), Charles allowed the magistrates and fifty-two guild leaders from Ghent to come before him to make their obeisance and symbolic apologies. According to an eyewitness, these supplicants were led from the square into the courtyard where they were kept waiting for almost two hours in the snow.[168] When called to enter the hall, each of these notables from Ghent was required to kneel three times on the ground with his guild's banner "unfurled before him on a lance"[169] and then to place the banner at the feet of Anthony, the Bastard of Burgundy, a powerful representative of the Valois duchy. Then, as an eyewitness noted, the entire group from Ghent "cried 'Mercy!' together very humbly, which was piteous to see and hear."[170] The entire list of earlier concessions was formally read aloud by the first secretary of Burgundy and dramatically swept away as he sliced the document in half in front of the entire convocation.[171] Charles the Bold followed this symbolic action with a formal listing of all offences perpetrated by the inhabitants of Ghent and ordered the re-closing of the city gates, the acceptance of the proffered banners and the cries for mercy, and the relinquishment of the previous privileges. He ended his harangue by promising to be a "good prince" if those from Ghent promised to be "good people and children as you ought to be."[172] The "hated *quellote* [taxes]" was subsequently restored and Ghent lost its civic autonomy with the installation of new leaders appointed by Charles' representatives.[173]

As humiliating as this public censure must have been, the townspeople of Liège suffered more mortal and devastating losses than did the people of Ghent as a result of their protests. Liège, as previously mentioned, was not one of Charles' territories but belonged to the Church, and had become, under Charles'

---

[167] See Vaughn, 7-9, for a detailed account of the convocation, a *précis* of which follows.

[168] Vaughan, 8. See also *Collection de documens inédits*, i. 204-9 and de Commynes, *Mémoires*, ed. Dupont, iii. 253-60.

[169] Vaughan, 8.

[170] Ibid.

[171] Ibid.

[172] Vaughan, 9.

[173] Ibid.

father, vocal in its criticism of the ascension of Louis of Bourbon as bishop. This vehement protest resulted in a declaration of war against Burgundy encouraged by Louis XI.[174] In a peace treaty signed in 1466, Charles became the "hereditary guardian" of Liège which was, in turn, required to pay an onerous fine to the duke, *each payment* of which was secured by the handing over of fifty hostages.[175] In spite of, or perhaps because of, this treaty, Liège continued to cause difficulty, with the rioting continuing under the leadership of Charles the Bold as the new Duke of Burgundy. After one victory, Charles responded dramatically by abolishing the constitution of Liège, stripping the city of its bishopric, tearing down its walls and gates, and disarming the city.[176] Richard Vaughan, in his account, notes that

> …[t]he peace settlement, or judicial sentence, dictated by Charles to Liège on 28 November 1467 was absolutist in character and more extreme, in its severity, than the similar settlement imposed by Duke John the Fearless in 1408 after the battle of Othée…[f]or Duke Charles's sentence abolished the laws and customs, the lawcourts [sic], indeed the entire civic constitution, of Liège.[177]

After further rioting by the Liègeois, Charles won a decisive victory in 1468 that resulted in the looting, burning, and demolishing of large sections of the city and the killing of much of the populace, leading Christine Weightman to note, with restraint, that Charles' "severity often amounted to brutality."[178] The extent of this brutality can be glimpsed in the letter that Jehan de Mazilles, the duke's cup-bearer, wrote to his sister concerning the crippling of Liège by Charles the Bold after that city's rebellion. Having reached the outskirts of Liège, Charles

---

[174] Vaughan, 11.

[175] Ibid.

[176] Vaughan, 24.

[177] Ibid.

[178] Weightman, 67. Weightman also cites Charles lauding his men's fighting in Nesle with the comment, "…[T]ruly I have good butchers with me" (67). In 1471, another act of savagery (of which there were many) found Charles the Bold and his army burning more than 2000 French towns and castles on his return to Burgundy after France refused to meet him in battle. Taylor, Aline S. *Isabel of Burgundy* (New York: Tempus, 2002), 212-213.

the Bold entered the city walls and met 16,000 to 18,000 combatants seeking to defend their city. Mazilles chronicles some of the ensuing carnage:

> Ever so many of their people were slain and drowned…. We flew to the market-place and the church of St. Lambert where a number of prisoners were taken and thrown into the water.[179] …All the churches – more than four hundred – were pillaged and plundered. It is rumored that they will be burnt together with the rest of the city. Piteous it is to see what ill is wrought…."[180]

In addition to this military action, Charles forced the destitute survivors of Liège to pay taxes and rents for the demolished property. Liège became a city under Burgundian control, curbed by the new duke's well-known ferocity, although it remained physically outside of Charles' territories.

Charles became renowned for his cruelty in Ghent and Dinant as well as in Liège, and these cities, in turn, persistently resisted him and his policies. Earlier, before his ascension as Duke of Burgundy, Charles had ably demonstrated his ruthlessness when he had had the leaders of Dinant tied back-to-back and thrown off the citadel after defeating that city. Such despotism caused widespread criticism because they proved Charles, in battle, to be no respecter of persons, punishing aristocrats as harshly as "ordinary criminals."[181] Word of Charles' cruelty in Dinant and Liège traveled through the Low Countries, prompting Ghent to submit in 1469 and Tournai to pay a tribute to avoid war.[182] These cities nonetheless continued to be two of the more independent cities in the duchy. In fact, the actions of powerful merchant communities such as these led Richard Vaughan to assert that "[t]he real enemy of Duke Charles the Bold, opposing him with a bitter and consistent hatred, was urban."[183]

---

[179] This action would usually result in drowning, with the "opposition" clothed, perhaps armed, and unable to swim.

[180] Jehan de Mazilles in Commynes-Dupont, Preuves, iii. 241-242.

[181] Weightman, 67.

[182] Weightman, 88.

[183] Vaughan, 40.

Margaret of York, a Powerful Duchess

From 1473 until his death in 1477 at Nancy, Charles was almost continually at war, and his absence precipitated Margaret's significant involvement in affairs of state as her husband's representative. Traditionally, Burgundian duchesses assisted with the administration of the duchy while their husbands were at war; Margaret, however, exceeded these expectations as Duchess of Burgundy and, later, as Dowager Duchess, as she aided her step-daughter, Mary, and son-in-law, Emperor Maximillian I. By 1474, Margaret was assigned the task of encouraging her brother, Edward IV of England, to invade France while Charles focused on a siege of Neuss in the Rhineland.[184] With her brother's acquiescence, Margaret assisted with the arrangements for the Burgundian ships that would transport an English army of at least 1200 men to the continent, met with Portuguese ambassadors, requested men for an army to fight the French in Artois and Hainault,[185] and later negotiated more than once with the cities of the Low Countries in order to levy more troops. She maintained a presence at Ghent to monitor the political mood of that volatile city[186] and successfully requested large sums of money from the cities in 1468 and again in 1475, an undertaking that she and Charles' daughter, Mary, were forced to repeat in a meeting of the *États Généraux* in 1476 after Charles became desperate for more appropriations to counter his disastrous military campaigns against the Swiss.[187] As Wim Blockmans has noted, Margaret became more influential politically as she assumed further administrative responsibilities:

> From 1475 onward, during the duke's lengthy absences, Margaret played a certain political role. She led the resistance against a

---

[184] For a comprehensive discussion of Margaret's activity, see Weightman, *Margaret of York*, 88-101. Weightman makes the point that "…[I]t is also clear from the behavior of powerful women like Isabell of Portugal and Margaret herself that women could and did act on their own authority and were expected to assume a wide range of responsibilities" (84).

[185] Weightman, 88.

[186] Ibid.

[187] Wims Blockman, "The Devotion of a Lonely Duchess" in *Margaret of York, Simon Marmion, and the Visions of Tonda.* For more on Margaret's strategic role in raising funds for Charles' military campaigns, see
Blockman, 31-32.

French invasion of Artois and negotiated with the Flemish cities for the mobilization of troops. In September 1475, she requested 18,000 *ryders* from the cities – this in addition to the 40,000 *ryders* she has been granted in 1468.[188]

In spite of the goodwill with which Margaret was regarded by Charles' subjects, her later 1476 request for further funds and troops was met with vehement opposition:

> … [T]he delegates resisted all the demands especially the ducal order for a further levy of 7,000 troops to be drawn from all the cities of the Low Countries. The Chancellor Hugonet met their refusal with anger and he threatened the estates with the wrath of the duke if they did not immediately comply with his demands. The session ended in uproar but Margaret continued to work behind the scenes and she managed to ensure more troops were sent to Lorraine.[189]

Margaret continued to support actively her husband's war effort up to the time of his disappearance at Nancy in 1477. At this time, Margaret and Mary urged the central *Chambre des Comptes* to continue their duties, summoned the *États Généraux*, protested the French claim to Saint-Quentin in a letter to King Louis of France, and publicly announced Charles' death on January 24, once they had received an eye-witness report of it.[190]

Margaret then worked diligently to preserve the duchy intact for Charles' heir, Mary of Burgundy, by again requesting funds from the *États Généreaux* to fight Louis XI who had seized upon Mary's vulnerability as an opportunity to reclaim lands from Burgundian control. Further, under great duress, Margaret also played a significant role in the successful arrangement of Mary's marriage to Maximilian of Austria, a match that had been negotiated in 1476. Although it took from January when Charles was killed in battle at Nancy to April of 1477

---

[188] Blockman, 31.

[189] Weightman, 100.

[190] Blockman, 31.

to conclude the marriage arrangements and bring about the union of Mary and Maximillian by proxy, the advantageous marriage, coupled with the populace's outrage at Louis XI's aggressive behavior at the time, brought stable governance to Burgundy once more.[191]

Margaret's political activity continued after Mary's marriage to Maximilian, a recognition that showed the emperor's appreciation of Margaret's political connections and influence. At the time of Charles' death, Margaret's dowry had been half-paid by her brother, Edward IV. Mary, now Charles' heir, fought for the full instatement of that dowry, despite its inadequate funding which invalidated her claims to the entire amount, stating reasons of "deep love and reverence" that Mary held for Margaret and Margaret's "perfect love and goodwill" with which she had held "our person and our lands and lordships."[192] As Weightman notes, restoring the complete dowry to Margaret would also increase her status and make her brother, Edward IV, more apt to aid Burgundy in defending its territories against French incursions.[193] In a defense of Margaret's importance to Burgundy, Mary noted that the dowager duchess was

> …fully occupied in dealing with the very high and very mighty prince, our well beloved lord and cousin the King of England, to persuade him to come to our aid and to uphold the everlasting alliances and treaties which were signed between him and our late lord and father.[194]

Margaret was, in fact, sent by Maximilian I on a diplomatic mission to England to negotiate another alliance between her native England and Burgundy, as Edward IV by this time had allied with the King of France. Just before her untimely death in 1482 following a hunting accident, Mary requested Margaret oversee the care of Mary's children, Philip and Margaret, an arrangement that

---

[191] Luc Hommel feels Margaret, by virtue of her role in these marriage negotiations, was "greatly responsible for the existence of the present-day kingdom of Belgium" in *Marguerite d'York ou La Duchesse Junon* (Paris: 1954) 111.

[192] Weightman 120.

[193] Ibid.

[194] Ibid.

ultimately involved Margaret's supervision of the education of Philip, Mary's heir.[195] Because of her close relationship with Mary, Maximilian, and their children, and because of her familial ties to the English throne, Margaret continued to possess significant influence as a dowager duchess, an influence she was careful to maintain and protect.

David Aubert and the Douce 365 *L'Abbaye de saint esprit*

David Aubert, the scribe for the Douce 365 version of *L'Abbaye du saint esprit* and *écrivain*[196] for Philip the Good, Charles the Bold, and Margaret of York, spent the greater part of his working life in the dissenting city of Ghent, among people who had felt firsthand the brutality of Charles the Bold. *Ecrivains*, as Patrick de Winter has observed, acted as more than professional copyists who merely transcribed works, instead resembling *stationnaires* with responsibilities that included, in the case of luxury texts, "the hiring of illuminators, miniature painters, and even binders, in addition to setting the layout of the book."[197] Aubert, as *écrivain,* would have been intimately involved in the production of the Douce 365 text which was commissioned by Margaret of York for her personal library.[198]

According to *A Summary Catalogue of Western Manuscripts in the Bodleian Library at Oxford*, the Douce 365 version of *L'Abbaye du saint esprit* dates to 1475,[199] a date that coincides with Margaret's increasing participation in Burgundian affairs of state, with the period of Aubert's patronage by Margaret of York (1475-76) as noted by Richard Straub,[200] and with Kurtis Barstow's dating of the manuscript to 1475-76.[201] That it would have been difficult for

---

[195] For a fuller discussion of the dynastic conflicts surrounding the rearing of Mary's children, see Weightman 139-142.

[196] Scribe

[197] Patrick de Winter, "The *Grandes Heures* of Philip the Bold, Duke of Burgundy: The Copyist Jean L'Avenant and His Patrons at the French Court," *Speculum* 57.4 (1982), 786.

[198] Falconer Madan, *A Summary Catalogue of Western Manuscripts in the Bodleian Library at Oxford* (Oxford, 1897), 607.

[199] Ibid.

[200] Straub in Cynthia Brown, Review, *Speculum* 71.3 (1996), 1033.

[201] Kurtis Barstow, "Appendix: The Library of Margaret of York and Some Related Books," *Margaret of York, Simon Marmion, and The Visions of Tondal* (Malibu, Getty P, 1992), 260.

David Aubert to have transcribed all forty-three manuscripts attributed to him by modern scholars leaves room to argue the presence of other hands in some of these works; however, the specific additions in the Douce 365, their intended reception by the Duchess of Burgundy, the presence of Aubert in Ghent at a time of high discontent with Charles the Bold's governmental policies, and the years of manuscript production that correspond to the most difficult period politically of Charles the Bold's reign, all argue for Aubert's production of the Douce 365 *L'Abbaye du saint esprit* with its dialogue and additions.

Other compelling reasons argue for Aubert's production of the Douce 365 manuscript that contains the *L'Abbaye,* its additional dialogue, and other treatises of devotion. First, the manuscript's codicil refers to Aubert as "son escripuain indigne,"[202] while making it clear that he wrote and organized the additional effects, including the four miniatures that enhance the Douce 365 manuscript:

> Here ends several very devout treatises…[from] the volume that was written and organized…at the request of the princess…Lady Margaret of York, Duchess of Burgundy…in the city of Ghent, in the month of March, the year of grace 1475, by David Aubert, its humble copyist.[203]

Further, in the fourth miniature of the Douce 365 manuscript, the *écrivain* David Aubert is depicted in the figure of Calyo. In the first of the fourth miniature's double images, Calyo receives the seventh treatise of the Douce 365 manuscript listed as *"Le Liure de Seneque intitule Des remedes contre les maulz de fortune…"*[204] from Seneca. In the second image, Calyo presents the seventh treatise to "Philip of Burgundy,"[205] a gesture that might presage Aubert's upcoming presentation of the manuscript at the Burgundian court.

---

[202] "Its humble copyist."

[203] "Cy finent aucuns moult devote traitties…lequel volume a este escript et ordonne…par le commandement de la princesse…madame Marguerite de Yorke, duchesse de Bourgoingne… en sa ville de Gant au mois de mars lan de grace Mil cccc soixante et quinze, par David Aubert son escripuain indigne" (Madan 607).

[204] "The Book of Seneca entitled *Remedies against the Vagaries of Fortune.*"

[205] Madan, 607. Because the manuscript clearly states that it dates to 1475 and Philip the Good died in 1467, it would make perfect sense for the recipient to be Charles the Bold. Madan,

Finally, David Aubert was more than qualified to produce the Douce 365 *L'Abbaye du saint esprit*, with its lengthy dialogue between Christ and *Fille* (Daughter/Soul). As the scribe to Philip the Good and Charles the Bold, Aubert would have been familiar with the 13th century *Grandes Chroniques de France*,[206] which creates a quasi-legendary history of France from the fall of Troy through the reign of Charles V (the great-great-uncle of Charles the Bold). The *Grandes Chroniques,* in seeking to promote France as the defender of Holy Church, maintains, according to Lori Walters, that the "French nobility's obligation to preserve learning was [to be] balanced by the duty of the educated to *guide the nobility*[207] in bringing about the realization of the City of God on earth – in France and in all of Christendom."[208] Further, as Luitpold Wallach has noted, Aubert's *Chroniques et Conquestes de Charlemaine* may well owe a debt to the *Grandes Chroniques*, as well as to such works such as the *Chroniques de Saint-Denis* or the Latin Pseudo-Turpin,[209] and Aubert could well have thought his Burgundian patrons would be most interested in bolstering their reputations as rulers by capitalizing on the religious nuances contained therein. Consonant with Walters' assertion above, Aubert, as scribe, could have hoped to exercise his "duty" as an educated man by guiding Margaret and Charles, in the tradition of the *Grandes Chroniques de France,* to respect France and the Church. Certainly, as we shall see in the following chapter, the additions found in the Douce 365 *L'Abbaye du saint esprit* reflect the apostolic and "incarnational politics"[210] of the period as the treatise emphasizes the moral

---

however, clearly states that the recipient is "Philip of Burgundy," making one assume this treatise had been first given to that duke and then copied and adapted for this particular collection.

[206] *The Grand Chronicles of France.*

[207] Italics added.

[208] Lori Walters, "The Royal Vernacular: Poet and Patron in Christine de Pizan's *Charles V* and *Les Sept psaumes allegorisés*" in *The Vernacular Spirit: Essays on Medieval Religious Literature*, eds. Renate Blumenfeld Kosinski, Duncan Robertson, and Nancy Bradley Warren (New York: Palgrave, 2002), 167.

[209] Madan, Falconer, *A Summary Catalogue of the Western Manuscripts in the Bodleian Library at Oxford* (Oxford: Clarendon, 1897) 607.

[210] Nancy Bradley Warren, "Introduction," *The Embodied Word: Female Spiritualities, Contested Orthodoxies, and English Religious Cultures, 1350-1700* (Notre Dame: U of Notre Dame P, 2010), 7. Warren predicates a masterful discussion of female spirituality in her text on the terms incarnational piety, incarnational epistemology, incarnational textuality, and incarnational politics. These terms are defined in her introduction.

seriousness of war against the King of France, God's "representative" on earth, and warns the Duchess of Burgundy of the spiritual dangers implicit in her political actions on behalf of her husband. This warning, in the additional dialogue between Christ and *Fille*, takes the form of a meditation in the first person and reflects the dissent prevalent in Ghent, Aubert's city of residence.

The Douce 365 *L'Abbaye du saint esprit* and Its Devotional Context

Margaret of York was a *devotée* of *Devotio Moderna,* a movement initiated through the preaching and *Resolutions* of Geert Grote of Deventer in the Ijssel river valley of the Low Countries.[211] The guiding principles of this movement, with its emphasis on humility, obedience to God's will, community life outside of a monastery, and personal meditation as the path to God, figure prominently in the themes of the Douce 365 *L'Abbaye du saint esprit,* which is attributed to 1475, a particularly turbulent time politically for Charles and Margaret. Brothers and sisters who practiced *Devotio Moderna* did not take formal institutional vows but lived together in committed religious communities intent on following and reclaiming apostolic purity in religious practice. The New Devout differed from the earlier Beguines and Beghards by eschewing individual ownership of property, thereby holding possessions in common, and by emphasizing the community to the point that sisters within their houses and brothers within theirs were to admonish each other and help each other progress in spiritual growth, much as the institutionally religious did in chapter meetings.[212] As John Engen has noted, "This orientation toward a community rather than an individual effort…affected the tone within each house,"[213] as the New Devout sought to live a life "in common."

They further emphasized the development of interiority in religious practice to the point that their work involved more a spiritual "becoming" than a

---

[211] John Van Engen, *Devotio Moderna: Basic Writings, Classics of Western Spirituality* (New York: Paulist P, 1988), 36. For detailed information on Grote and the *Devotio Moderna,* see pp. 7-61 of this text. I am indebted to Van Engen for his description of *Devotio Moderna.*

[212] Van Engen, 18.

[213] Ibid.

charitable "doing." The emphasis here centered on developing a profound relationship with God that would result in Christ-like behavior.[214] As a result, the Modern Devout sought to cultivate spiritual virtues through reflection on one's own habits and motives for action, and to fortify positive virtues through individual spiritual exercises that heightened interiority.

Because Geert Grote, through his *Resolutions,* held this interiority to be essential to a vital spiritual life, the Modern Devout came to view asceticism and other outward exercises as a hindrance to the believer's knowledge of God's love. In his "Sermon Addressed to the Laity," Grote went so far as to say, "In seeking these three [righteousness, peace, and joy in the Holy Spirit], a man should let every external religious exercise go."[215] Private meditations, based on scripture, the Church fathers, or continual prayer, became the primary devotional activities for followers of the movement, and these meditations were considered appropriate for lay persons residing outside of a cloister or religious community, including those individuals who were married.

The New Devout emphasized foremost the practice of humility through individual exercises that often included subjecting members to "humiliating work, admonishment, discipline or other spiritual tasks to remove...traces of personal pride"[216] in order to cultivate Christian virtues. Foremost among these personal exercises was the contemplation of the Passion of Christ, a widespread practice during the later Middle Ages that encouraged the believer to identify with Christ more fully and individually:

> ...the result or purpose of [the meditation on Christ's Passion] was ideally fourfold: to "relive" with Christ his virtuous life and saving passion, to have him ever present before one's eyes, to

---

[214] Van Engen notes that Modern Devotion emphasized "constant meditation, especially meditation on Scripture or scriptural images, but with an end that was neither sensational nor mystical but rather a deepened interiority expressed in holy conduct" (44). For a discussion of differences between beguines and devotées of *Devotio Moderna,* see Van Engen, 18-19.

[215] Geert Grote, "A Sermon Addressed to the Laity," *Devotio Moderna: Basic Writings, Classics of Western Spirituality,* trans. John Von Engen (New York, Paulist P, 1988), 92.

[216] Van Engen, 32.

manifest his presence to others, and to orchestrate, as it were,
one's mental and emotional faculties around devotion to him.[217]

In these respects, the New Devout echoed practices found in institutional
orders within the Church while differing from these groups in expressing their
individual commitment via their own individually written resolutions rather
than through the institutional vow. Because of their appreciation of interiority,
the New Devout, while seeking to lead a pure apostolic life, did not focus on
outer charitable works; rather, they worked on their individual spiritual lives and
the cultivation of virtue while supporting themselves through such occupations
as book production (undertaken most often by the men) and brewing as well as
manufacture of textiles (undertaken most often by the women, although some
women did textual copy work).[218]

Geert Grote himself did not seek so much to establish a movement as he
sought to turn from his formerly hedonistic life which he described as involving
"fornicat[ion] on every hilltop and under every spreading tree."[219] To effect this
conversion, Grote wrote a series of personal resolutions which he adopted as
guidelines for his new spiritual life, considering these writings to be personal vows
made privately before God. [220] Following Grote's example, the New Devout committed themselves to resolutions that they, in turn, privately and individually drew
up, pledging themselves before God to live according to scripture and their own
spiritual resolutions. Those desiring to join the New Devout made no formal institutional vow; were not required to have money, property, or education; nor needed
or to be single in order to join. This lack of institutional vow figures prominently
in the foundational reason for the creation of the later versions of *L'Abbaye du saint
esprit* presently under consideration,[221] as the treatise claims as its audience those
devout, uncloistered souls who seek to create an abbey of the "conscience" as an aid

---

[217] Van Engen, 25.

[218] Van Engen, 24.

[219] Geert Grote, *Letter 23, Gerardi Magni Epistolae,* ed. W. Mulder (Antwerp, 1933) 105-106,
qtd. in Van Engen, 37.

[220] Van Engen, 40.

[221] The 14th century Royal 16E.xii *L'Abbaye* and the 15th century Douce 365 treatise.

to living the "mixed" life.[222] It is important to note that while participating actively in *Devotio Moderna*, the New Devout continued to worship at their local churches and followed the practices that were part of expected religious expression.[223]

Religious works, especially those related to the Desert Fathers, were translated by the Modern Devout in an effort to present them in the vernacular for use in personal devotions. Here again, the practices of the Devout mirror the structure of the Douce 365 *L'Abbaye* as it cites throughout the treatise significant religious writers, such as saints Paul, Gregory, Bernard, and Denis; and instructional scripture concerning the kings David, Solomon, and Nebuchadnezzar. With an emphasis on encouraging Christian virtues, the Devout also translated works by Bonaventure, Gregory the Great, Anselm, William of St. Thierry, and Hugh of St. Victor into the vernacular (in this case, Middle Dutch).[224] These vernacular texts provided the basis for collations, open meetings held by the Devout in which the public could be admonished and quietly proselytized. The public's growing respect for the New Devout resulted in an increasing number of believers seeking to improve their spiritual relationship to God via reading, contemplation, and prayer.[225]

In light of these guiding principles of *Devotio Moderna*, Chapter 4 will seek to explicate the effect of contemporary influences, born of Burgundian politics and of Margaret's religious preferences, upon the Douce 365 *L'Abbaye du saint esprit*. Margaret's' dedication to the precepts of *Devotio Moderna*; her sincere piety which sought to establish, maintain, and reform convents, particularly those of the Poor Clares, and monasteries of the Franciscans and Augustinians; and her dedication to the Church, influenced the additions singular to the Douce 365 treatise. Her *écrivain*, David Aubert of Ghent, a city much abused by Charles the Bold's policies, fulfilled Margaret of York's commission for a copy of *L'Abbaye du saint esprit*. In doing so, he made several short additions to the text while also

---

[222] A pious life lived outside of a monastery.

[223] Van Engen, 15.

[224] Van Engen, "Introduction" to *Devotio Moderna: Basic Writings,* 40. As mentioned in Chapter 1, Hugh of St. Victor was at one time considered the original author of *L'Abbaye du saint esprit.*

[225] One of the most famous of the followers of *Devotio Moderna* is Thomas à Kempis, who is almost universally viewed as the author of *The Imitation of Christ,* a work born of the discipline of meditation and interiority, activities that were foundational to Grote's religious practice.

including a significant 352-line dialogue between Christ and *Fille* (Daughter) not found in any other redaction of this treatise. These additions taken together deepen our understanding of the milieu in which Margaret of York lived with the constant political turmoil, continual requests (especially for ecclesiastical reform), and ever-pressing obligations expected of the devout duchess who held herself to the highest standards. In the Douce 365 *L'Abbaye du saint esprit*, we find a vivid vignette of Margaret's life, rendered in terms of the religious views she held most dear.

CHAPTER 4

ADDITIONAL DIALOGUE AND ADMONITIONS IN THE DOUCE 365 *L'ABBAYE DU SAINT ESPRIT*

The Douce 365 *L'Abbaye du saint esprit* participates in the purging and establishment of virtues in the hearts of those living a religious life outside of a cloistered religious order. It is, above all, an "incarnational" text, one that is meant to create a "clean heart" within the reader, as the psalmist prayed in Psalm 50:12,[226] and to mold the reader into a new person in Christ, in the spirit of *imitatio Christi*. The purpose of *L'Abbaye du saint esprit,* that of creating a metaphorical abbey of the heart to aid the reader in embodying Christ-like virtues and priorities, is consonant with the focus of *Devotio Moderna* and reflects Margaret of York's preferences in religious instruction. The Douce 365 treatise, which Margaret commissioned, is therefore exceptionally well poised to appeal to the new Duchess of Burgundy, reflecting as it does her dynastic responsibilities and her commitment to *Devotio Moderna* with its exercises meant to inculcate Christian virtues.[227]

As Wim Blockmans has suggested, the Douce 365 *L'Abbaye* may well have been given by Margaret to Charles the Bold as a wedding present so that both of them could enjoy it as a devotional aid. It appears to have also been meant as a potential instructional tool for Marie of Burgundy, Charles the Bold's daughter

---

[226] *The Holy Bible,* Douay-Rheims, 2007. See also Psalm 51:10 I King James Version. The Douay-Rheims Bible will be used throughout this chapter.

[227] Weightman notes that Margaret and her mother, Cecily Neville, were adherents of *Devotio Moderna* and that Margaret's dedication to the movement was "both personal and public." Margaret also maintained contact with "Denis van Rijkel, a Carthusan scholar and teacher, [who was] one of the leading theologians of the Low Countries" (198).

by an earlier marriage and Margaret's charge. Margaret most probably knew the treatise in an earlier form in England while under the influence of her devout mother, Cecily Neville, and indeed, the Douce 365 version of the treatise appends the English ending to the French text. As we shall see, the English ending of the Douce 365 *L'Abbaye* serves to reinforce the political message of this expanded text, a message Margaret might well have deciphered, given the frequent use of subtle and instructive allegory in medieval texts meant for aristocratic audiences.

Since the earliest French manuscript, Yates Thompson 11, dates from c.1300 and consequently precedes Geert Grote's experiences of c.1375 that mark the beginning of the *Devotio Moderna* movement, the earliest version of *L'Abbaye de saint esprit* appears not to have been written with the Modern Devout who were seeking to live a religious life outside of the cloister in mind. The Douce 365 *L'Abbaye,* however, with its attribution of 1475,[228] falls well after the time of *Devotio Moderna*'s beginnings with Grote's *Resolutions,* making possible the introduction of that movement's tenets into the Douce 365 treatise. Further, in a treatise commissioned by and for Margaret of York, the addition of such devotional material would have been entirely appropriate, appealing, as it would have, to the Duchess of Burgundy, a self-professed follower of the movement.

Devotio Moderna, which emphasized individual cultivation of a spiritual life, also advocated reform of established convents, a project which Margaret embraced enthusiastically. For thirty-five years, Margaret actively pursued religious reform in the Low Countries "reform[ing]… the church, founding and refounding convents, building churches and monasteries and giving generously to the church."[229] She was drawn especially to the teachings of the Augustinians, possibly because of the preferences of Denis van Rijkel, and founded a convent of Augustinian nuns.[230] Margaret also established several hospitals and orphanages as well as schools and hostels in the Lowlands, in addition to a home for "reformed prostitutes, known as the [D]aughters of Magdalen."[231] Possibly because

---

[228] Falconer Madan, *A Summary Catalogue of Western Manuscripts in the Bodleian Library at Oxford* (Oxford: Clarendon, 17), 607.

[229] Weightman, 199.

[230] Weightman, 199-200.

[231] Weightman, 200.

she was barren, Margaret particularly favored the Poor Clares to whom she gave a "lavishly illustrated Vie de Sainte Colette"[232] which is still extant.

To analyze more clearly the Douce 365 *L'Abbaye du saint esprit* as a vehicle adapted for Margaret's use and for presenting certain political messages by the scribe David Aubert to the royal reader within the context of *Devotio Moderna*, we will first consider key words located frequently in texts associated with that devotional movement, then discuss additional addresses of *Fille* (Daughter) added to the Douce 365 *L'Abbaye du saint esprit,* and finally analyze an additional 352-line dialogue between Christ and *Fille* found only in the fourth redaction of the treatise. This lengthy dialogue relates to both Margaret's religious preferences and to the political turmoil associated with Charles the Bold's reign, and provides evidence of the scribe's interest in adapting the devotional treatise for royal consumption during a turbulent time in Burgundian history.

Key Words Often Found in Texts
Associated with *Devotio Moderna*

John Van Engen, in his introduction to the basic works of *Devotio Moderna* translated from Middle Dutch, identifies eleven terms which occur repeatedly in the writings of the New Devout.[233] From these terms, Van Engen composes a list to aid in locating significant aspects of the movement beyond the most numerous and expected terms, "Jesus" and "Christ." The first few key words he lists, *conversio* and *resolutio*, are ones that appear integral to a number of religious movements; yet, in the context of *Devotio Moderna,* these terms carry specific and varying connotations. For the New Devout, *conversio* conveyed a "turning toward the Lord" that was viewed as a lifelong, "continuous process" and a "way of life."[234] There was, Van Engen writes, "no fascination with the moment or the means" of conversion, but instead, *conversio* denoted a "taking up" of this

---

[232] Weightman, 200. St. Colette had worked with the Poor Clares in the fifteenth century and was canonized in the early nineteenth century (200). She is the patron saint of women unable to conceive and of sick children.

[233] John Van Engen, *Devotio Moderna: Basic Writings*, The Classics of Western Spirituality (New York: Paulist P, 1988), 28-34.

[234] Van Engen, 28.

new path on the journey toward developing a faithful relationship with Christ.[235] *Resolutio* referred to the specific resolutions drawn up by each individual believer which were viewed as a contract between him and God, rather than a more general interpretation of "resolving to be faithful." These two terms formed the foundation of New Devout spirituality in which no formal institutional vows were taken. To make a set of resolutions indicated that an individual meant to participate in the New Devout movement and to submit to God's will rather than her own.

Another term integral to the practice of the New Devotion, *exercitium*, refers to the exercises that were meant to inculcate in the individual believer virtues represented by four other frequently mentioned words: *caritas* (Christian love), *humilitas* (humility), *obedientia* (obedience), and *puritas* (purity). While these spiritual exercises might involve ascetic acts, the New Devout were focused not on asceticism but on *profectus virtutum*, the believer's growth in spiritual virtues.[236] With the absence of formal vows, the exercises themselves became "the practical manifestations of a good resolve" and served, in the most successful cases, to guide the practitioner into a deeper connection with, and commitment to, the Divine.[237]

Through the practices of conversion (turning toward God), resolution (the "contract" with God), and exercises to encourage spiritual growth, the ultimate goal of *Devotio Moderna*, that of *Puritas cordis* (Purity of Heart), could be held secure in the believer's mind. As Van Engen notes, this goal represented an ideal "not reachable finally in this life" while stemming from "Jesus'… promise [that] [t]he pure in heart will see God."[238] In the texts of *Devotio Moderna*, the frequently-used references to *cor* denoted the "innermost part of a person" and provided a way of addressing "the [intangible] God-given core of every person,"[239] while *affectus* acknowledged the desires, emotions, and impulses that needed to be directed in positive ways in order to cultivate a pure heart, "full of godly affections and goodly desire [that] was the goal of [this] way of life."[240]

---

[235] Ibid.

[236] Van Engen points out that "the notion of exercise was not original with them;" yet, the "New Devout gave it an emphasis… rarely or never found earlier" (30).

[237] Ibid.

[238] Van Engen, 34. See also Matthew 5:8.

[239] Van Engen, 33.

[240] Van Engen, 34.

One of the exercises used early in the conversion process consequently included *momento mori*, the contemplation of death and the ensuing process of decay that was meant to impress upon the initiate the shortness of time remaining in his lifespan and the necessity of beginning immediately to develop a virtuous life.

L'Abbaye du saint esprit, especially when viewed in light of its specific additions, stands as a vehicle uniquely situated to carry these spiritual ideals as well as political suggestions to its royal reader. As an essentially incarnational work, *L'Abbaye du saint esprit* seeks to prepare its stated audience of the uncloistered devout, to house a pure soul, concomitantly rendering the believer's body the container, or "Abbey," of that Holy Spirit. The Douce 365 *L'Abbaye*, in containing significant additions over the previous redactions, carries this purpose forward for its specific audience by presenting eight addresses directed to *Fille* [Daughter] in the fourth redaction of the treatise to one direct address of *Fille* in each of the earlier three redactions of the text.[241] Further, the Douce 365 text includes a passage on good governance that is interrupted by the extensive, additional dialogue between Christ and *Fille* unique to this fourth redaction of the treatise. In this dialogue, *Fille* expresses intense personal remorse in the first person and participates in a meditation using *momento mori*. This additional 352-line dialogue, which also references the Passion of Christ, ends with an admonition against the hypothetical capture of the king of France and denounces those who would condone such a nefarious undertaking. It is my contention that the scribe Davide Aubert of Ghent presented these additions to the Douce 365 *L'Abbaye du saint esprit*[242] in terms consonant with the tenets of *Devotio Moderna* in order to seek Margaret's aid in ameliorating the suffering in the Low Countries carried forward by the policies of her husband, Charles the Bold, and begun previously by his father, Philip the Good. As far-fetched as it may seem, Charles the Bold, with his blood-soaked politics, can reasonably be considered a

---

[241] See the end of Chapter 1 above for Chesney's discussion of these four redactions.

[242] The fourth redaction of the text includes both the Douce 365 *L'Abbaye du saint esprit* and the Vesoul 91 treatise which Chesney finds to be a copy of the Douce 365 *L'Abbaye*. This copy evinces the same planning throughout although it lacks the final embellishments and miniatures. Chesney concludes that both treatises "emanated from the same workshop" (16).

possible reader of the Douce 365 *L'Abbaye* for, despite his well-known arrogance, cruelty, and violence, he prided himself on being quite devout.[243]

Additional Addresses of *Fille* in the Douce 365 *L'Abbaye du saint esprit*

The rhetorical device *"Ha Fille,"* found eight times in the Douce 365 *"L'Abbaye du saint esprit,* begins with an interjection that can be translated variously as *"Ha!"* or "Ah!," words that are meant to call the reader's attention particularly to the passage at hand.[244] Similar in purpose to the phrase "Listen, Daughter!" (*Audi filia*), "Ha Fille" marks a passage of particular significance in a written work and references the feminized Soul (the spiritual Anima) as viewed in Psalm 44:11-12.[245] Because a passage introduced by "Ha Fille" was purposely set apart for particular emphasis, it is significant that the Douce 365 *L'Abbaye* contains seven additional uses of the phrase over the one such address in previous French redactions of the treatise. These are passages in the Douce 365 *L'Abbaye* worthy of closer examination in light of the treatise's specific creation for Margaret of York and Charles the Bold. The injunction to "Listen, Daughter and see" found at the beginning of Psalm 44:11 encourages spiritual insight through textual engagement as do the seven additional addresses of "Ha Fille" within the Douce 365 *L'Abbaye.* By including these addresses in a work commissioned by Margaret of York, the scribe emphasizes passages that are consonant with *Devotio Moderna* and that frequently urge Margaret to consider her obligations to refine her soul as Christ's Beloved while helping to restore peaceful interactions in the realm.

---

[243] Vaughan notes Charles the Bold was "deeply religious in the traditional sense and yielded to no other prince in piety and devotion" (161). See "the Ruler and His Court" in Vaughan (156-196).

[244] *"Fille,"* however, takes on an added dimension in a treatise commissioned by a woman as was the Douce 365 *L'Abbaye.*

[245] "Harken, O daughter, and see, and incline thy ear: and forget thy people and thy father's house. And the king shall greatly desire thy beauty; for he is the Lord thy God, and him they shall adore" (Ps. 44: 11-12).

THE FIRST ADDITIONAL ADDRESS

The first four additional addresses of *Fille* out of the seven found in the Douce 365 treatise occur in passages of narrative shared by the first three redactions of the French treatise; however, these early French manuscripts do not include these four specific direct addresses. The remaining three of the seven additional direct addresses occur only in the 352-line dialogue between Christ and *Fille* that is unique to the Douce 365 (fourth) redaction of the treatise. The first four additional addresses using "Ha Fille" are the simplest of the seven added to the Douce 365 *L'Abbaye du saint esprit*.

Traditionally glossed as a call for the Soul as Bride to prepare to meet the Bridegroom Christ, "Ha Fille" in the first additional address occurs after the initial purgation of the soul at the hands of the allegorical ladies Truth and Love of Purity, and before the building of the Abbey's foundation. After the conscience is purged, Humility makes the foundations "bas et parfons" while Poverty renders them "grans et larges,en largement donner quanques elle poeult tenir et avoir "(fol. 1v, ll. 25-27 – fol. 2, l. 1). [246] At this point, the first additional address occurs: "Ha a fille, beneoite soit la religion qui est fondee en pourete et en humilite. Cest encontre aulcune maulvais religieux orguerilleuz et convoitteuz" (fol. 2, ll. 1-4).[247] Truth and Love of Purity join Humility and Poverty as attributes advocated by *Devotio Moderna*[248] that contrast with the actions of those professed religious who are "proud and covetous," a warning that will occur later in the additional dialogue.

After the abbey is established by Poverty and Humility, and situated on the river of Mary Magdalene's repentant tears, Obedience and Mercy come to build its walls "grans et haulz" (fol. 2v, ll. 21-22).[249] The Douce manuscript makes

---

[246] "Low and deep, large and wide...generously giving whatever she might possess and have."

[247] "Ah, Daughter, blessed be the religion that is founded on poverty and humility. This is the opposite of any falsely religious (people) who are proud and covetous." This warning could reference both the professed religious who have taken institutional vows as well as those readers of the treatise who spiritually consider themselves to be dedicated religious.

[248] As we have seen above, John Van Engen finds *Humilitas* to be one of the words frequently found in writings of the New Devout, making it clear that humility was needed to turn toward God (*conversio*) and proclaim intent to submit one's will to the Divine (*resolutio*).

[249] "Great and high."

it clear that these are the walls of religion and that one must act with mercy and compassion toward the poor (fol. 2v, ll. 22-23), a conviction it associates with Christ's commandment to love one another: "…Je vous donne ung nouvel commandement cest que vous amez lun laultre ainsi que je vous ayme…" (fol. 2v, ll. 24-26).[250] *Fille* is also advised, according to Douce 365, to consider "le conseil de nostre mere sainte eglise" (fol. 2v, ll. 1-2),[251] advice which appears in earlier redactions without a reference to the Church as "our Mother." Following these guidelines will result, in this redaction, in an edifice as impressive as that of "Saloman," and in the Holy Spirit coming to live within the abbey of one's conscience (fol. 2v, l. 5).

The placement of the address directed to *Fille* in connection with poverty and humility and the further additional description of Holy Church as "our Mother," neither of which are found in the French manuscripts of earlier redactions, take on further meaning when considered in light of Charles' 1474 taxation of church lands and property. In the *Les Grandes Chroniques de France*, the original chronicler, Primat, a monk from the royal abbey of Saint-Denis, uses the metaphor of a daughter caring for her mother to represent France as the defender of Holy Church.[252] The king of France, as the head of the body politic and the physical embodiment not only of Divinity but of France itself, was to be held responsible for preserving learning and promoting the welfare of the Church. Charles the Bold, an aspirant to kingship, far from preserving the church, created hardship with his policies of taxing church lands and property. As opposition grew, clerical lawyers sought to prove the new taxes illegal, and while Charles eventually collected a great deal of the tax, resentment of his taxation policies remained among the populace. This first direct address, then, and the additional reference to "our Mother, Holy Church," emphasize a need for humility and mercy as well as filial obedience to the Church, significant advice for Margaret and Charles to read in light of Charles' recent actions.

---

[250] "I give you a new commandment: Love one another as I have loved you."

[251] "The advice of our Mother, Holy Church."

[252] Lori Walters, "The Royal Vernacular: Poet and Patron in Christine de Pizan's *Charles V* and the *Sept psaumes allégorisés*," *The Vernacular Spirit: Essays on Medieval Religious Literature*, eds. Renate Blumenfeld_Kosinski, Duncan Robertson, and Nancy Bradley Warren (New York, 2002), 172.

With respect to the addition of "our Mother, Holy Church," there exists the possibility of another three-leveled interpretation. First, *Fille,* as Soul and as daughter of "our Mother, Holy Church," owes allegiance to the ecclesiastical hierarchy, emphasizing the necessity of obedience and humility. The family dynamics in this passage imply that the readers, Margaret of York and Charles the Bold, have a filial obligation to adhere to the Church's teachings and obey its admonitions to humility, poverty, obedience, and mercy. On a theological level, the relationship of Daughter to Mother Church parallels the soul's relationship to Christ and the responsibility of the devout to embody the Incarnation through construction of an interior cloister of the soul.[253] On a third, more political level, the ruler, in caring for the church as a daughter would a mother (as Primat suggests), is encouraged by the text to temper justice with mercy, a virtue being explicated in this passage. Charles the Bold would be a plausible target for such counsel, with his determined focus on unifying his holdings into a powerful kingdom, his ruthless treatment of those who disobeyed his edicts, his taxation of Church lands and property, and his continuous demands, through Margaret, for financial and martial support of his military campaigns.

The ensuing vows of poverty, chastity, and obedience in the Douce 365 *L'Abbaye* allow for another, more nuanced interpretation of these vows to reside within the devotional treatise, thereby subtly reinforcing other directives for obedience found in the additional dialogue with Christ. In a similar manner, *Fille,* as an accepted address of a woman ecclesiastic by a superior, when applied to a secular individual such as the Duchess of Burgundy, serves to remind the duchess of a higher, spiritual allegiance and of her own subordination to the ecclesiastical hierarchy, a subordination the devout yet ruthless Duke of Burgundy is also enjoined to share.

THE SECOND ADDITIONAL ADDRESS

The second additional use of *"Ha Fille,"* appears within a passage advocating "guarding one's cloister," a firm injunction emphasizing physical and spiritual purity through enclosure of the senses. Again, French manuscripts in the first three redactions *of L'Abbaye du saint esprit* do not contain this additional direct

---

[253] This view recalls Origin's interpretation of the Beloved in the Song of Songs.

address of *Fille*, although they contain this passage advising the reader to "gardes bien ton clostre" (f. 3, ll. 16-17) in order to maintain an enclosed body and be truly religious: "[B]aisses et cloz tes yeulz et te abstiens de legierement regarder. Tes oreilles du mal daultruy oys. Ta bouche de trop parler et rire. Cloz ton coeur encontre toute mauvaise pensee" (fol. 3v, ll. 17-21).[254] Passages advocating the strict guarding of the five senses permeate medieval devotional treatises, as in the twelfth-century *Speculum virginum* where the enclosure centers on the containment of women by limiting their spatial freedom and opportunity for sensual experience. These exhortations to maintain a kind of spiritual cloister take on a new sense of urgency, however, when the abbey under construction resides metaphorically within the reader's own body, as Janice Pinder has noted: "When the spiritual life has no other location than the subject's body, it is the body itself that must be enclosed."[255] Under the guise of traditional and allegorical monastic enclosure, Douce 365's second additional direct address of *Fille* further highlights containment as a necessary pathway to purity while foreshadowing Christ's later accusations of *Fille* as materialistic, greedy, and sensual in the later, additional dialogue. With this address, the tradition of enclosure that evokes the *hortus conclusus* of the *Song of Songs* and the enclosure of the Virgin's body transfers subtly to the more secular purpose of limiting the future political actions of the intended readers, in this case the Duke and Duchess of Burgundy, by sanctioning the enclosed body of the contained woman or Christian king, careful to remain "untainted" by worldly affairs.

THE THIRD AND FOURTH ADDITIONAL ADDRESSES

The third address directed to *Fille* that is not found in manuscripts of earlier redactions, reminds *Fille* that this "is a holy abbey and a good religion" in which dwell such "holy…personages" as the abbess Charity, the prioress Wisdom, and sub-prioress Humility: "ha doulce fille que cy a sainte abbaye et bonne religion

---

[254] "Guard your cloister…Lower and close your eyes and abstain from looking lightly; [close] your ears from hearing evil about others, your mouth from speaking or laughing too much. Close your heart against all bad thought."

[255] See Janice Pinder, "The Cloister and the Garden," in Constant Mews, *Listen, Daughter*, for a discussion of religious and spiritual enclosure.

ou il a et demeure si vaillans gens si saintes et si dignes personnes et ou il a si souffissant abbaesse comme charite prieuse comme sapience et soubz prieuse comme humilite" (fol. 4v, l. 26 – fol. 5, l. 3).[256] The fourth address of *Fille* states that those who follow these three allegorical figures are blessed and that their lives are ordered and regulated charitably, sagely, and humbly: "fille beneoittes soient les nonnains qui bien gardent les commandemens de charite les consaulz de sapience et les enseignemens de humilite et qui toute leur vie meneront ordonneront et riegleront charitablement sagement et humblement" (fol. 5, ll. 3-8).[257] These two direct addresses of *Fille* in the Douce 365 *L'Abbaye du saint esprit* occur within a passage that concerns itself with good governance in the tradition of the *miroir des princes* and stresses the ordering of a kingdom to promote political peace. This section is longer and more elaborate than that found in the courtly Royal 16E.XII *L'Abbaye* of the third redaction and advises the reader how to usher in a period of civic joy and repose by ruling with Charity, Wisdom, and Humility. The passage is preceded by a quotation from the Psalms attributed by the text to David,[258] traditionally viewed in France as a prototype of the Christian king, and continues with a vignette from the life of Nebuchadnezzar, the king described biblically as needing to recognize God's sovereignty.[259]

The story of Nebuchadnezzar raises interesting parallels with the behavior of Charles the Bold as he continues in his quest for political glory and, to that end, demands crushing financial and human sacrifices of his subjects. In the fourth chapter of the book of Daniel, Nebuchadnezzar has a dream that Daniel interprets to mean that Nebuchadnezzar will be banished from his kingdom and made to live as a beast of the field because he has believed all of his power and wealth are the result of his own achievement. Daniel informs him that unless he

---

[256] "Sweet Daughter, this is a holy abbey and good religion in which dwell such valiant people, such holy and worthy personages, and where there are so capable an abbess as Charity, a prioress as Wisdom, and an sub-prioress as Humility."

[257] "Daughter, blessed are the nuns who keep well the commandments of love, the counsels of wisdom, and the teachings of humility, and who, all their lives, will lead, order and regulate charitably, wisely, and humbly."

[258] "…And the Most High himself hath founded her [the Church]" (Psalm 86:5).

[259] "They shall cast thee out from among men and thy dwelling shall be with cattle and with wild beasts…till thou know that the most High ruleth over the kingdom of men and giveth it to whomsoever he will" (Psalm 4:22).

becomes humble and repents by being generous to the less fortunate, he will not regain his throne. True to this prophetic dream, God casts Nebuchadnezzar out of Babylon and causes him to live as a beast until the king realizes that all his blessings come from God. After experiencing a change of heart, Nebuchadnezzar regains his throne and praises God, at which point the author of the book of Daniel warns the reader that "them (sic) that walk in pride, [God] is able to abase."[260] Nebuchadnezzar's story, then, serves a warning against pride and neglecting God who is the source of the king's blessings.

It is significant that the Douce 365 additional dialogue between *Fille* and Christ is inserted in the midst of this passage that emphasizes the role of humility, wisdom, and charity in good governance, and that the third and fourth addresses directed to *Fille* highlight the quotations presented above. After the additional dialogue, which we will discuss below, the discussion of Nebuchadnezzar's later, spiritual governance continues and promises that the realm ordered by Wisdom, Charity, and Humility shall experience "ne plaits ne noises mais joye et paiz" (fol. 11v, l. 2)[261] Such a kingdom will be appropriately blessed: "beneoit soit le royaulme et la religion qui est faite et ordonnee par charite par sens et par humilite" (fol. 11v, ll. 3-4).[262]

Given the duress experienced by many in Charles the Bold's kingdom in 1475-77 because of his unbridled ambition, the political dissent fomenting in Ghent where Aubert is working, and the responsibility of a scribe to instruct a king for the good of the country,[263] it is not surprising that the Douce 365 text contains two direct addresses of *Fille* at this point, emphasizing the qualities necessary for responsible leadership. It is also significant that this redaction includes the very powerful abbess Charity which all French redactions mention but which the Douce 365 treatise develops more fully, and that the additional dialogue between Christ and *Fille*, found only in this redaction of the text, has been placed in the middle

---

[260] Daniel 4:34.

[261] "...no complaints, no disputes, only joy and peace."

[262] "Blessed be the realm and the religion that is made and ordered by Charity, by Wisdom, and by Humility."

[263] As scribe to Philippe the Good and Charles the Bold in the tradition of *Les Grands Chroniques de France*, David Aubert was expected to instruct the ruler out of his informed perspective as a trustworthy scribe.

of the admonitions given through the narrative of Nebuchadnezzar. Further, the additional dialogue between Christ and *Fille* found only in the fourth redaction begins on line 8 out of twenty-eight lines on folio 5v in the Douce 365 version with no change in handwriting, precluding the possibility of the accidental binding of loose leaves from an unrelated manuscript. After the additional dialogue, the treatise returns on line 9 of folio 11v to its discussion of Nebuchadnezzar. The inclusion of two direct addresses in the passage preceding the dialogue between Christ and *Fille*, the mention of a powerful abbess, and the extensive, additional passage with its overtones of guilt which follows, argue for the Douce 365 scribe's intent not merely to present a text but to adapt it for its influential reader.

Another Attempt to Influence Margaret of York

Before considering the 352-line additional dialogue of the Douce 365 *L'Abbaye du saint* esprit, it might be helpful to note that the attempt by a scribe to reach Charles through Margaret, as well as to influence Margaret herself, is not a unique occurrence during this period, as evidenced by a treatise in Add. Ms. 7970, another manuscript written for Margaret and housed in her personal library.[264] In the Add. Ms. 7970 treatise, *Le Dialogue de la Duchesse de Bourgogne à Jésu Christ,*[265] the scribe, Nicholas Finet, tells Margaret, through the first-person voice of Christ, that she must do whatever she can to reform the cloisters and enforce regular observance, especially among the four mendicant orders responsible for preaching:

> You shall do all that you can, which will be for the common good,
> in all your affairs, especially in the spiritual state of the church,
> so that the cloisters might be reformed and the regular observance

---

[264] London, British Library, Add. Ms. 7970, fols. 3r-140v. The dialogue in this manuscript represents an entirely different work than that between Christ and *Fille* in the Douce 365 "*L'Abbaye du saint esprit.*"

[265] "The Dialogue of the Duchess of Burgundy with Jesus Christ."

might be invigorated, the same as with the four orders of the mendicants who have to preach to others…..[266]

Finet then warns Margaret that if she declines this challenge by saying she is weak, she should consider her powerful and wise husband who can and must exhort others to help in this cause: "Et se tu me dis que tu es flaibe de corps et ia anchienne de tamps, tu as ton mary prince trespuissant saige et vaillant lequel peulz et dois enhorter poindre et embraser pour acconplir ce que dit est (fol. 99v, l. 5 – fol. 100, l. 2).[267] The scribe states further that, if necessary, the duke can petition the Pope for the necessary authority to reform the cloisters: "…ne me dyes quil na point de pooir ne iuridicion sur les gens deglise par quoy ne les poroit contraindre tu le dois enhorter quil obtiengne auctorite depar nostre saint pere le pape sur les dittes personnes pour les reformer…" (fol. 100, l. 3 – fol. 100v, l. 2).[268] That Margaret is clearly viewed in this passage as a means of access to Charles is significant. Clearly, David Aubert is not the only scribe inserting advice meant for Margaret into a religious manuscript.

Douce 365's Additional Dialogue between Christ and *Fille*

While the previously discussed additions to the Douce 365 *L'Abbaye du saint esprit* emphasize the qualities of charity,[269] obedience, humility, and wisdom in the living of the saintly life, the lengthy additional dialogue that follows calls for the purification of the reader, *Fille*, so that these qualities may dwell once again in human form. In a meditation centering on the Passion of Christ, a key

---

[266] "Tu feras ce que poras qui en toy sera pour le bien commun en tous tes affayres principalement en lestat de leglise et espirituel affin que les cloistres soyet reformes et la reguliere observance soit en vigeur meismement es quatre ordes des mendians qui ont a preschier aux aultres…" (fol. 98v, l.10 – fol. 99, l.12).

[267] "And if you tell me that you are weak in body and aged, you have your husband, a very powerful, wise, and valiant prince, who can and must exhort, goad, and inspire in order to accomplish that which is said."

[268] "And don't tell me that he has no power or jurisdiction over people in the church by which he might constrain them. You must exhort him to obtain authority on behalf of our Holy Father the Pope over said persons in order to reform them."

[269] *Caritas.*

exercise of *Devotio Moderna*, Christ presents an account of his suffering and torment in the first person.

The additional dialogue begins, in the middle of the extended passage on good governance discussed above, with the assurance that the Trinity will comfort and aid those rulers who govern charitably, sagely, and humbly, although it states that the world will despise them: "Le pere le filz et le saint esperit les confortera et aidera mais le monde les despitera" (fol. 5v, ll. 8-9).[270] While detailing Christ's sufferings, this section presents the remaining three additional direct addresses of *Fille* in the Douce 365 treatise. Using the first person voice, Christ tells the reader not to be dismayed by the world's rejection as Christ was tormented on earth, and the reader cannot expect to be treated more kindly than he was. He reminds "ma chiere fille" that Christ's life was lived "en pourete en tribulation en meschief en angoisse en durete et en toute asprete" (fol. 5v, ll. 13-15)[271] and reviews the torments of his life, reminding *Fille* that the persecution didn't begin with his death but reaches as far back as Herod's Slaughter of the Innocents. He reminds her that he only lived thirty-three years, and that he was condemned and crucified. Continuing this litany of sacrifice, Christ informs *Fille* in the final two address that no cord or nails could have bound him to the cross if it had not had been God's will and that all this suffering was undertaken on her behalf. His great love for her, Christ explains, tied him to the cross: "... mais le tres grant amour que jauoie a vous ma chiere fille et le tres grant fam et soif que jauoie de vostre salut ce fut le souuerain lyen qui a la coulompne me lya et qui a la croiz me cloua et soustint par mes deux mains en layz" (fol. 6, ll.19-24).[272] Love and concern for *Fille*'s well-being constituted the "supreme bond" that "tied Christ to the column and nailed him to the cross."

Fille's remorseful response to Christ that follows is designated in the chapter heading as belonging to the nuns of the abbey or the "world," here indicating those devout souls who are not cloistered physically: "Comment apres plusieurs

---

[270] "The Father, the Son, and the Holy Spirit will comfort and aid them but the world will despise them."

[271] "...in poverty, tribulation, distress, agony, hardship, and in all difficulty."

[272] "...but the very great love that I devote to you, dear daughter, and the very great hunger and thirst I declare for your salvation, this was the supreme bond that fastened me to the column and nailed me to the cross, and was endured by my two bound hands."

belles remonstrances les nonnains del abbaye et religion du saint esprit cest a entendre le monde doibt recognoistre la grant charite que ihesucrist notre seigneur a eu a nous" (fol. 6, ll.25-28).[273] The dialogue that ensues contrasts Christ's selfless sacrifice with the spiritual vacuity of *Fille* (the soul and the reader whom Christ has addressed in the first person), and *Fille* is reminded that, by "lauctorite de dieu le pere," Christ is the "souuerain Juge des humains" (fol. 7, ll. 20, 21).[274] This designation adds biblical force to an already solemn parental dialogue between "Father" and Daughter, while the representation of the soul as *Fille,* who answers Christ in the first person, aligns with the female reader, Margaret of York, thereby subtly encouraging the duchess to internalize *Fille*'s thoughts as if they were her own.

Continuing in the first person voice that encourages the reader's entry into *Fille*'s guilt and need for salvation, *Fille*'s dialogue acknowledges her unhealthy spiritual state and need for redemption. She finds that Christ has been her "shield [that] was suspended and cruelly mutilated in the service of [her] defense" so that she could be "completely reconciled" to God.[275] *Fille* considers Christ's Passion and her own hardness of heart that has not cracked and split as did the stones that witnessed his crucifixion. She acknowledges that all good comes from God and notes that no one enjoys blessings because of her own talents or innate worth, an obvious echo of Nebuchadnezzar's lesson concerning pride which this dialogue interrupts: "...tous ceulz et toutes celles[276] q[ui] telz biens ont...les doibuent tenir de vous [Christ] sans nul aultre et non point croire ne penser que ils en possessent par leur sens ou par leur vertu ou vaillance..." (f. 7v, ll. 22-26).[277] Echoing Nebuchadnezzar's fall from grace, *Fille* further notes that there are many people

---

[273] "How after many beautiful demonstrations, the nuns of the abbey and religious order of the Holy Spirit, that is to say, the world, must bear witness to the great love that Jesus Christ, our Lord, had for us."

[274] "The authority of God, the Father...sovereign judge of humans."

[275] "...esai fut perchie et cruellement mutille ou service de ma defense," "vous eustes mon pere a moy du tout appaise..." (f. 7, ll. 14-16, 17-18).

[276] Note that "those" is written in both masculine and feminine forms.

[277] "...all those [m. and f.] who have such blessings must hold them from you [Christ], not from any other, and [must] not at all believe or think that they possess them by their own intelligence or by their virtue or valor."

of "great lineage and sagacity"[278] who fail to acknowledge God as the source of their blessings and therefore become "corrupt and vulgar."[279] It is against this backdrop of implied guilt that *Fille* begins a lengthy confession of her own sinful and proud behavior.

It is not surprising given the implications of guilt contained in this dialogue that *Fille*'s sins are extensive and relate directly to the previous additional addresses of *Fille* in the Douce 365 *L'Abbaye*. These earlier addresses, taken together, call on *Fille* to live with humility and in poverty, and to act sagely and charitably. It is precisely these admonitions that *Fille* violates, according to the catalogue of sins that ensues (fol. 8, ll. 4 - f. 8v, l. 18). *Fille* acknowledges, again in the first person, that she is ungrateful for her many privileges and has not shared her blessings with others: It has pained her to spend five *sous* on the welfare of others in Christ's name while she will spend lavishly on baubles for herself (fol. 8, ll. 13-15). She would rather please herself than please God and has consequently averted funds meant to be used for others' needs (f. 8, ll. 4-9), an accusation that takes on new meaning when we consider Margaret's requests for large sums of money from the cities of the Low Countries for her husband's military campaigns. She has been proud of her parentage (fol. 8v, ll. 8-11), a reference that coincides with Margaret's station in life, and rather than use the blessings that have accrued from her social position for the benefit of others, she has used them to please herself and to furnish her body with worldly pleasures (ll. 16-18). Because of the example she has set, her vanity has put others on the road to "eternele dempnation" (fol. 9, ll. 16-17).

At this point, *Fille* participates in *momento mori*, another exercise popular in *Devotio Moderna,* by meditating on her physical decay in death, realizing that her beauty will not help her and that her "obstinee perversite" is "en tous temps contrarie" to Christ's goal and the gifts of the spirit (fol. 9, ll. 21-22).[280] In misery, *Fille* asks Christ to leave her until she is able to comprehend fully the innumerable blessings she has enjoyed and the love for her that Christ has exemplified.

---

[278] "moult de grans lignaiges et sages gens" (fol. 7v, ll. 26-27).

[279] "pource et malostrue" (fol. 7v, ll. 27-28).

[280] "Obstinate perversity," "at all times contrary...."

She once more contrasts Christ's poverty and sacrifice to her desire to live all her life "en richesses en honneurs et en delices" (f. 10, ll. 22-23).[281]

According to these accusations, *Fille*'s sin lies in her failure to participate morally in the Incarnation, and her fleshly decay provides tangible evidence of that failure. In a work concerned primarily with embodying the Divine through the creation of a spiritual abbey in one's conscience, *Fille*'s failure to represent Christ aligns her with the fleshly, corruptible side of the physical/spiritual binary. As Françoise Jaouen and Benjamin Semple have noted, the human body, as a locus of both carnal sin and of spiritual incarnation, represents a site that is "at once threatening and exalted, a place of exile and a promised land."[282] This mixture of holy and worldly, the situation in which *Fille* finds herself as she seeks to be religious but enjoys worldly pleasures, threatens a basic tenet of the treatise, that it is possible for one to live a religious life without belonging to a holy order. The anxiety that attends this proposition is reflected in the treatise on three levels, that of the individual believer, the church, and the realm. As Caroline Walker Bynum has discussed in *Metamorphosis and Identity*, *mixtio*, viewed as medieval hybrid, remains an entity that, in Bernardian exegesis, never quite transforms into a new, stable entity, but remains dual while bringing together an uneasy combination of opposites.[283] Worldly pleasures and the religious life within the individual believer are viewed as separate entities with the potential, particularly in the case of the mixed life or the *vita apostolica*, for the spiritual life ultimately to be subsumed by the worldly. This anxiety can be found at the heart of criticisms surrounding individual approaches to religion and exists as the underlying tension of *L'Abbaye du saint esprit* that expresses itself in a fear that spiritual interiority may obviate the need for the institutional church. The appeal of the world for *Fille* is further reflected in her cosmetically enhanced visage and her love of baubles, a symptom in the treatise of moral disintegration, and

---

[281] "Riches, honor, and delight."

[282] Francoise Jaouen and Benjamin Semple, "Editor's Preface: The Body into Text." *Yale French Studies* 86 (1994), 3.

[283] For a discussion of *mixtio*, see Caroline Walker Bynum in *Metamorphosis and Identity* (New York, 2001), 117-43. Bynum notes, "even martyrs are "mixed," for "no one is free from sin in this life..." (121).

represents one of the anxieties surrounding the uncloistered spiritual individual in the world.

The moral disintegration of the individual (*Fille*) from a monastic standpoint is clear in this section and is reflected in her physical degeneration as well: "Je laisse moy mechante; je ay par moult defoiz plaint et regrette tant quil sembloit que fort il m'en pezast…. Elas moy tres chetifue creature et playne de presumption. Combien chargie me sens de grant desloiaulte…" (f. 8, ll. 17-19, 21-23).[284] Moral weakness in *Fille* no longer constitutes a solely individual threat, for according to the logic behind the *miroir des princes*, spiritual disintegration in a ruler stands to threaten the moral integrity of the country. Clearly, more than the individual soul is at stake when *Fille* is royal and in a position of political influence. This, of course, is the case with Margaret of York for whom the Douce 365 *L'Abbaye du saint esprit* was written and, by extension, with her husband Charles the Bold, both of whom have lived lives full of riches, honors, and delights, and appear, at least politically, not to exemplify the qualities of humility, charity, obedience, and wisdom that Christ requires of the Soul (*Fille*) in this dialogue. Because of her vain and worldly life, *Fille* has failed to embody Christ at the most basic level, and is therefore called upon to repent and establish a spiritual abbey in her heart.

In the Douce 365 *L'Abbaye du saint sprit,* the portrayal of *Fille* embracing worldly pleasures textualizes the anxieties associated with constructing a spiritual religion of the heart and with maintaining an allegorical cloister against the world. This anxiety extends to the individual spiritual person who lives in the world and has become part of it, perhaps to the detriment of her spiritual commitment.

Further, the accusations against *Fille* in the additional dialogue recall Margaret's political situation in Burgundy. She might also be accused of pride of parentage as an English princess, misuse of material wealth meant to further the common good through the solicitation of funds for military campaigns (not to mention the owning of jewels and preferment through royal honors), and depending on one's political view, "ungodly" leadership by supporting Charles

---

[284] "I wear myself out, being evil; I have so much reproach and regret for it [her sin] that it seems that it heavily weighs me down…. Woe is me, very miserable creature and full of presumption. How burdened I feel from great disloyalty…."

the Bold's worldly ambitions. As *Fille*'s catalogue of sins lengthens, it reaches its climax in a discussion of potential regicide, cited below, that the text describes as tantamount to a second crucifixion of Christ and that correspond with Margaret's levying of funds for war in her husband's absence, Charles' taxation of church property, and Burgundy's war against Louis XI in the attempt to create a Lothringian middle state. The exhortation to repent, found at the end of the additional dialogue, recalls the earlier admonitions to act humbly, sagely, and charitably, and emphasizes the relationship of those virtues to civil harmony, thereby linking the additional dialogue to the passage on Nebuchadnezzar and good governance. *Fille*'s decadence places economic and spiritual burdens on her subjects, and her reform would similarly reach beyond her own personal salvation to benefit the commonweal.

After cataloguing her sins in the first person, *Fille* compares her love of great honors and baubles to Christ's life of torment and poverty, and then makes a pointed and unforgettable comparison between the King of France and Christ:

> Certainly, if it came about that the king of France proceeded to some country in his kingdom and its inhabitants took him prisoner, deserting him and laughing and slapping (him) without any pity, (and) then they bound and battered him, and finally, led him to hang from the gallows without deserving it at all, those who would do this could not reasonably be called devoted and loyal men who certainly knew their king or their lord to have been made to endure and sustain such very great humiliation and suffering without having deserved it at all – to have him so cruelly and inhumanely treated as to put him wrongly to such a very cruel and villainous death, tyrannically usurping from him royal honors and ceremonies – Truly, many would consider such people to be insolent and lost.[285]

---

[285] Certes se il aduenoit que le roy de france se transportast en aulcune contree de son regne et les habitans de icelle le constituassent prisonnier puis le alaissent degabant et buffiant puis sans pite nulle le loiassent et batissent et finablement le menassent pendre au gibet sans aulcune desserte ceulz quy ce feroient pas ne se deburoient par raison nommer ses hommes liges et feables quy bien scauroient leur roy ou leur seigneur auoir fait endurer et soustenir si

After this passage, the additional dialogue ends with a statement that these are the lessons that the religious of this holy abbey must learn, and that they must repent and humble themselves in order to climb the mountain of tranquility. The passage on good governance that cites David and Nebuchadnezzar, earlier interrupted by the additional dialogue then continues, again promising peace and tranquility to the one who will order his life and his realm according to Charity and Humility.

This hypothetical situation concerning "King of France" is rather abruptly placed within the dialogue, being used ostensibly as an illustration that contrasts *Fille*'s privileged life and Christ's life of torment. After this metaphor, the text ends rather abruptly with the call for repentance. The lack of contextual continuity between the additional dialogue taken as a whole and the rest of the Douce 365 *L'Abbaye* suggests this passage portraying the King of France as a prisoner of war constitutes an urgent warning against disrespecting the divinity of kings, especially in a time of political hostilities, which, as we have seen, is the case in Burgundy at the time this manuscript was prepared. The capture of the King of France was a very real possibility in the war between Charles and Louis XI, and the aligning of the King's person with that of Christ occurs easily within the context of the *Grandes Chroniques de France* and within the traditional belief of the king as God's representative on earth. The warning itself is fitting for David Aubert to have made in his role as scribe to the Duke of Burgundy, as the responsibility in the tradition of the *Grandes Chroniques* lay with the king to protect the church and the learning associated with it, and with the scribe to instruct the ruler out of the informed perspective that he might have cultivated while enjoying the king's patronage. Further, the warning extends to the passive observers of such actions, judging them to be, if not accomplices, at least guilty bystanders. Thus, the passage appears to warn indirectly Margaret who, though not physically engaged in battle, actively supported it on Charles' behalf. At the same time, the dialogue warns Charles of the danger of ignoring the people's needs, of demanding yet more and more appropriations and troops, and of creating a political situation in which the King of France might well be killed or imprisoned.

---

tres grant vitupere et douleurs et sans aulcunement le auoir desseruy, le auoir tant cruellement et inhumainement traittie comme de a tort le mettre a mort si tres cruelle et villaine en luy tiranniquement usurpant les honneurs et les sirymonies royaulz. Certes moult deburoit ung tel poeuple estre tenu pour fol et pour desuoie (fol. 10v, ll. 6-22).

Further, the dialogue's intrusion into a discussion of Nebuchadnezzar and his later, godly governance, could well remind the medieval reader of that king's trials related in the fourth chapter of Daniel in which Nebuchadnezzar's overarching pride causes him to ignore God's benevolence and assume his good fortune and wealth to be a result of his own achievement, a pitfall ascribed to *Fille* in the additional dialogue. The swift punishment for this sin leaves the king bereft of reason and power, feeding on grass as do the wild beasts, only to be raised again to power when he, with humility, recognizes God's benevolence and divine sovereignty.[286]

The warnings implied in this passage and in the additional dialogue relate to contemporary political concerns of the House of Burgundy: Charles' almost continual engagement in costly battles against the King of France; Margaret's service as Charles' political representative at home; the public dissent that had become widespread and vocal, particularly at Ghent where Aubert resided; the exorbitant taxes burdening the populace during this time; and the alliances that other European princes had formed against the Duke of Burgundy. Adding to the widespread concern over Charles' brutality that exceeded that of his father Philippe the Good was the perception on the Continent that England, which offered (rather limited) military aid to Charles' enterprises during this period, was a "land of anarchy, violence, and blasphemy, where consecrated monarchs could be set aside at the whim of the rebellious nobility."[287] Considering this viewpoint, Margaret's support of Charles' actions, and Charles' violent, even bloodthirsty tactics, it is certainly possible that David Aubert, as royal scribe, could well have inserted the unique additional dialogue, found only in this redaction of *L'Abbaye du saint esprit*, with Margaret of York and Charles the Bold in mind.

Further, the additional dialogue's first-person meditation on Christ's Passion with the included recognition of *Fille*'s shortcomings and the final comparison of the King of France's death to that of Christ offers an oblique yet possibly effective psychological tool for admonishing and guiding the reader. The popularity of this

---

[286] See especially Daniel 4:22 (Douay Rheims): "They shall cast thee out from men and thy dwelling shall be with cattle and with wild beasts: and thou shalt eat grass as an ox and shall be wet with the dew of heaven: and seven times shall pass over thee, till thou know that the most High ruleth over the kingdom of men and giveth it to whomsoever he will."

[287] Weightman, 90. Weightman observes that the exile of Margaret of York's brother, Edward IV, was perceived by many on the continent as confirmation of this view.

genre of meditation allows for the rather subtle placement of key advice without coercing the reader or needlessly endangering the scribe, prudent considerations given the circumstances. Indeed, as events in France reached a crescendo and threatened the logical conclusion of death or imprisonment of a king, scribal adaptations with additional direct addresses of *Fille* and a dialogue between that "Daughter" and Christ may well have been viewed as one of the few ways to influence the Duchess of Burgundy and possibly the Duke, directly.[288] To ignore the rising discontent and the effect of Charles' decisions on his subjects could well have been more dangerous than to risk presenting the uncomfortable truth for the Duke and Duchess' consideration.

After the additional dialogue between Christ and *Fille*, the text briefly references the "ordering" of Nebuchadnezzar's governance[289] so that his kingdom might dwell in tranquility and then returns to the version of *L'Abbaye du saint esprit* found in the other manuscripts before adding its final direct address of *Fille*. Commenting on the waking of the religious for *matins*, the treatise points out to *Fille* that the alert soul is blessed: "Ma Fille, que benoitte soit lame que amour entiere dilligamment esveille ne quy point nest endormie ne parresseuse…" (fol. 15, ll. 2-4).[290] The treatise then makes a reference to the *Canticles*, saying that the heart awakens with the ardent love of God.

The disastrous results of not remaining diligently alert become obvious as the believer's soul is soon tested through the attack of the four daughters of the devil, known as Envy, Pride/Presumption, Murmur/Detraction, and False Judgment of Others. These daughters represent an inversion of the four daughters of the God (Wisdom, Mercy, Truth, and Justice) found in early French Passion plays such as Eustache Marcad's *La Passion d'Arras*, dating from the early fifteenth

---

[288] In *Les Visions du chevalier Tondal*, a treatise for which David Aubert was also the scribe (c.1475 in Ghent) and which was also commissioned by Margaret of York for her personal library, the knight Tondal is told that "those who want to be kings or emperors, not to uphold goodness but to reign over others, will suffer the great torments of those who are in the pit of Hell with Satan himself." Madeleine McDermott and Roger S. Wieck, Trans., "The Visions of Tondal: Text and Miniatures," *The Visions of Tondal* (Malibu, 1990), 52.

[289] The ordering occurs through the governance of Charity, Wisdom, and Humility.

[290] "My daughter, blessed be the soul that perfect love diligently awakens, that is not at all asleep or slothful…."

century.[291] This final direct address, then, admonishes the reader to be alert and act with the love of God, advice that corresponds to the message given by earlier textual additions.

The Douce 365 *L'Abbaye* and a Final Addition

Following the climactic struggle with the four evil daughters and the subsequent rescue by the Holy Spirit, the Douce 365 *L'Abbaye du saint esprit* avoids the various endings of the other French manuscripts in favor of a lengthy conclusion apparently borrowed from the English ending of the treatise that Margaret might well have encountered before her marriage. After reordering the allegorical abbey to restore it spiritually, the treatise pleads with "tous et toutes"[292] to be "dilligens et dilligentes[293] a vostre pouoir que chascune des bonnes dames quy en cestuy present traittie ont este nommees fachent espirituellement leur office chascun jour en voz coeurs" (fol. 16, ll. 18-19, 20-23).[294] The Douce 365 *L'Abbaye du saint esprit* then gives a final, additional warning also not present in earlier redactions of the French manuscripts: "Et bien vous gardez que point ne trespassez la regle de la religion ne lobedience des souuerains" (fol. 16, ll. 23-5).[295] This warning against disobeying the "sovereigns,"[296] here a reference to the allegorical *figurae* representing virtues in the text, recalls the admonition concerning the King of France, thereby subtly reinforcing that metaphor's sanction against traitorous action while underscoring the responsible behavior already emphasized by the seven additional direct addresses of *Fille* and by the additional dialogue between *Fille* and Christ.

---

[291] See Paula Giuliano, Introduction to *The Mystery of the Passion of the Third Day* (Asheville, North Carolina, 1996), ix.

[292] "all" (written in masculine and feminine forms).

[293] "diligent" (masculine and feminine forms).

[294] "...diligent [male and female forms] in your apprehension so that each one of the good ladies who has been named in this present treatise might make her office spiritually each day in your hearts."

[295] "And guard yourselves well that you do not at all violate the Rule of the religious order nor the obedience of the sovereigns."

[296] This use of "the sovereigns" in the Douce 365 *L'Abbaye* comes from the English *Abbey of the Holy Ghost* which Margaret knew in England.

The fuller conclusion given by Douce 365 brings the treatise to formal closure by elaborating key points in *L'Abbaye*: it reaffirms the location of the religion in the conscience; reviews the idea that the principles of the 'good ladies' must dwell in one's heart in order for this religion to remain secure; and instructs the reader, who is addressed in the second person imperative, to invoke the Holy Spirit's aid in times of temptation. It further reminds the reader of her power and stresses obedience to the rules of both religion and sovereigns, here again meaning spiritual leadership of the *figurae* while subtly reinforcing its more political message abjuring regicide. Finally, in securing the conscience as the temple of the Holy Spirit, it places this religion of the heart within an unarguably sanctioned and revered context.

The additional direct addresses of Fille found in the Douce 365 L'Abbaye du saint esprit unique to the fourth redaction of the French treatise, taken together, weave a pattern of subtle nuance and suggestion that serves to adapt an existing religious text for a political purpose: the admonition of Fille to follow the advice of "nostre mere sainte eglise,"[297] the pointed emphasis on obedience, the lengthy dialogue between Christ and Fille highlighting her shortcomings, and the comparison of an embattled King of France with Christ. These additions serve to reframe the incarnational message of L'Abbaye du saint esprit and to focus it on Margaret of York and the contemporary political conflicts between France and Burgundy, while the text itself prefigures the possibility of the Incarnation occurring within the individual reader through the coming of the Holy Spirit to the metaphorical abbey and the resulting purification that renders the Word "flesh" in the devout believer's body. That Fille fails to embody the Incarnation threatens the spiritual welfare of others to the point of hypothetical regicide and underscores the danger of her spiritual decadence to the commonweal. It is consequently not surprising, then, given the political climate that prevailed during its preparation, that the Douce 365 L'Abbaye du saint esprit, commissioned by Margaret of York as a wedding gift to Charles the Bold and created by the scribe David Aubert, closes with the English texts' admonishment for the reader to obey the "sovereigns" and that it represents the only redaction of the French texts to do so.

---

[297] "Our Mother, Holy Church."

CHAPTER 5

A MODERN ENGLISH TRANSLATION OF THE DOUCE 365 *L'ABBAYE DU SAINT ESPRIT*[298]

The Royal 16E.xii *L'Abbaye du saint esprit*, included in Chesney's third redaction of the treatise, dates to the fourteenth century and was apparently written for an aristocratic audience as evidenced by its elevated language, elaborate examples, and extensive use of allegory. This version of the treatise delineates its audience as those who would like to be "in religion," as are the professed religious, but cannot be because of certain limiting factors:

> Many people would like to enter into religion and are not able to because of poverty or because they are held by the bonds of marriage or for another reason. For these [people] is made a book so that those [m. (cil) and f. (celes)] who cannot enter into temporal religion may be in religion spiritually. [299]

This statement of intended audience has led to the belief that the *initial* audience for *L'Abbaye du saint esprit* included neither cloistered nor professed religious. The further direct address of *Fille* (Daughter) in later redactions has also led to the erroneous belief that the initial audience was female. This designation of audience does not consider that the earliest extant French redactions,

---

beginning with the Yates Thompson manuscript dating to c.1300, do not mention either of these parameters concerning audience; without that specific mention, the earliest audience for the treatise opens up to include, potentially, cloistered men and women.

Additionally, with the fourteenth-century Royal 16E.xii *L'Abbaye*, the stated audience is also designated as the devout male or female as indicated by the personal masculine and feminine pronouns *cil* and *celes*,[300] used to indicate those who desire to participate in the spiritual life. Further, redactions of the treatise that include the address of *Fille* (Daughter) have often been cited as having been written for a female audience exclusively. Because *Fille* can designate the "Soul" in Bernardian exegesis, however, the *L'Abbaye du saint esprit* resists this overly-simplified classification of its initial audience. Consequently, the very earliest readers of the extant c.1300 Yates Thompson 11 treatise[301] could have been cloistered males or females who would have found the architectural metaphor of the Abbey of the Holy Ghost reinforced daily by the setting in which they lived.

With the Royal 16E.XII treatise of the third redaction, *L'Abbaye du saint esprit* moves from the exclusive purview of the professed religious to those men and women interested in living a deeply spiritual life without taking institutional vows. With this statement of intent, the audience of the third redaction could and most probably did include a variety of devout individuals: beguines, the Modern Devout, and members of the nobility, including at least one king.[302]

The Douce 365 *L'Abbaye du saint esprit* of the fourth redaction derives from the Royal 16E.XII treatise and continues that version's use of elevated language and elaborate illustrations as well as extensive allegory. The Douce 365 treatise, commissioned by Margaret as a gift to Charles the Bold upon their marriage in 1469, contains significant additions over the earlier Royal 16E.XII redaction: seven additional direct addresses of *Fille,* a 352-line dialogue between Christ and *Fille,* a

---

[300] "Those"

[301] Yates Thompson 11 (formerly Add. Ms. 39843) dates from c.1300, according to *The Catalogue of Additions to the British Museum, 1854-1860*, 211.

[302] Both Add. Ms. 29986 and Ms. Bibliothèque Royale 9555-58 are stated to have belonged to "Jean, Duc de Berry," while Ms. Royal 16E.XII contains the initials "H.R.," possibly representing Henry VII or Henry VIII. *Catalogue of Additions to the British Library, 1876-1881*, 16; *Catalogue des manuscrits de la Bibliothèque royal de Belgique*, 409; *Catalogue of Western Manuscripts in the Old Royal*, 198.

warning against potential regicide committed against a French king, and an ending taken from an earlier English version of the treatise. The additional dialogue interrupts a discussion of good governance through the practice of Charity, Sagacity, and Humility, and recounts Nebuchadnezzar's loss of a kingdom through hubris. It then moves to a meditation on the Passion of Christ, an inventory of *Fille's* sins, and a self-examination through the use of *momento mori,* all exercises practiced in *Devotio Moderna,* a movement that Margaret of York embraced enthusiastically. The listing of the reader's (*Fille's*) sins culminate in the passage of hypothetical regicide of the French king after his capture in battle, a distinct possibility considering the ongoing battles between that king and Charles the Bold.

The ensuing condemnation against those who would kill the anointed representative of God and the admonition to obey the "sovereigns" borrowed from the English treatise, taken together, serve to reinforce the political messages of the additional dialogue included by the scribe from Ghent, David Aubert. These messages illustrate the appropriation of a devotional treatise in order to advise its powerful readers in the tradition of *Les Grandes Chroniques de France*, thereby opening a window on the social and historical *milieu* in which the Douce 365 *L'Abbaye du saint esprit* was written.

Translation and Editorial Methodologies

The translation of the Middle French Douce 365 *L'Abbaye du saint esprit* seeks to maintain the original sentence structure as closely as possible while presenting a readable modern English version of the text. French idiomatic structures were adapted during translation, however, and sentences are broken into more manageable lengths, usually at the point of a conjunction. Modern punctuation has been added to enhance the text's readability. Where an additional word is needed for clarification, it has been added in brackets. Where a passage is obscure, the original French passage is given in the chapter notes.

The rubrics of Douce 365 have been maintained with their introductions of each chapter and with their faulty, and then non-existent, numbering.[303] When

---

[303] The chapter numbers of the Douce 365 treatise become inaccurate, until finally after the last numbered chapter (fourteen, which in reality is chapter sixteen), the scribe simply indicates

a word has been given in the original French in both its male and female forms, that word is followed in the English translation by [m. & f.].[304] This notation allows the reader to consider the intended audience's gender in the French original.

Chapter notes are included for textual commentary and reference, and the English translation of the Latin Vulgate was used for biblical references.

Modern-English Translation of the Douce 365 *L'Abbaye du saint esprit: The Abbey of the Holy Spirit*

Here begins a beautiful treatise of old, compiled by master Jean Gerson, Doctor of Theology[305] which is entitled *The Abbey of the Holy Spirit*.

First Chapter: How each person may found this abbey in his conscience.

I see that many people would like very much to be in religion but they may not because of poverty or because they are held by ties of marriage or for another reason. And for so many, a religion of the Abbey of the Holy Spirit is made in the heart so that all those who are not able to be in religion[306] physically may be in religion spiritually. Ah, beautiful Lord God, where will this religion be founded and this abbey established? Truly, I say, in a place which is called the conscience.

We have often seen, and certainly it has happened, that today in this beautiful and noble place of preachers and minor friars, in such a place that customarily would be very foul and uninhabitable, there it happens spiritually that the Holy Spirit wishes to work. Now, it is necessary, first of all, to purge and clean the place, that is to say, the conscience, of all filth, all thorns, and all thistles so that the place may be well-suited for the founding of so noble and so high an edifice as the Abbey of the Holy Spirit.

---

the beginning of a new chapter with the words *"Le Chapitre."*

[304] Indication of male and female.

[305] This designation is doubtful for two reasons: (1) the earliest manuscript of *The Abbey* dates to 1300 and Gerson lived so from 1363-1429, and (2) the Douce 365 treatise dates to c.1475, some 46 years after Gerson's death. The ascription probably seeks to lend ecclesiastical authority to *The Abbey*. See Chapter 1, pp. 22-23.

[306] Here, "in religion" connotes taking institutional vows to join an established order.

Chapter Two: How the Holy Spirit, in order to enclose his abbey with good walls, shall send the ladies Truth, Love of Purity, Humility, and Poverty there.

Before, then, this will be done, the Holy Spirit sends two brave, valiant, and wise ladies there. The first is Lady Truth and the other is named Love of Purity. And for as many as will be in the abbey, they will guard the heart from all impurity and all evil thoughts so that shame will never be so great that they [the impurities] could become governesses of the habitation. When the place of the conscience is completely purged, it is necessary to make the foundations wide and deep. This the two ladies will do (that is to say, Humility and Poverty). Humility makes the [foundations] low and deep, and Poverty makes them large and wide, and casts the earth out, here and there, generously giving whatever she may possess. Ah, Daughter,[307] blessed be the religion that is founded on poverty and humility. This is the opposite of any falsely religious people who are proud and covetous.[308]

Chapter Three: How the walls of this abbey are raised by two ladies, Obedience and Misericord, and how by two other ladies, Patience and Strength, the pillars are set up, fastened, and established.

This religion, then, must be found on a good river of tears and crying because the village, city, or abbey that is situated on a good river is more comfortable and lovely. The Magdalene was founded on a good river, so great good came from it.[309] And this is what the prophet said: *Tanquam lignum quod plantatum est secus decursus aquarum.*[310] And in another place, he said, *Fluminis impetus*

---

[307] "Daughter" (*Fille*) represents the individual's Soul as well as the female reader (Margaret of York) who, with her husband Charles the Bold, is the scribe's intended reader.

[308] While a commentary on unspiritual clergy, this line also introduces the two dominant shortcomings for which *Fille* is chastised later in the treatise. Although this commentary exists in other redactions of the treatise, in the Douce 365 manuscript, it appears to serve additionally as a foreshadowing technique.

[309] The river of tears represents repentance, while "Magdalene" references Mary Magdalene who, in the Middle Ages, was considered a repentant prostitute.

[310] Psalm 1:3. Citations are taken from the Latin vulgate Bible.

laetificat ciutatem dei.[311] The good river makes the city clean, connected, secure, and abundant in merchandise.[312]

Lady Obedience, on the one hand, and Lady Misericord, on the other, make the walls of the religion great and high in generously giving to the poor through the mercy and compassion which one has from her Parent,[313] in obedience to our Lord who said, "I give you a new commandment. It is that you love one another as I love you."[314] Every time that we do good works for the love of God, by his commandment, and by the counsel of our mother the Holy Church, and every time that we give alms, we put so many good stones in our edifice and in our wall.

We read that Solomon made his house of very great, precious stones from which the habitation of the Holy Spirit must be made.[315] These are great and devout works of charity and all good works that must be joined together with good vitality and great warmth. But what is such vitality and great warmth if not love of God and of his nearest relative [his son] that joins one love to another and one good work to another? But so that the wall might be good and long-lasting, it is necessary that it be made of good cement. And what is that strong cement? True Faith. Thus says David, *Omnia opera eius in fide.*[316] All works, he says, must be [undertaken] in faith. And all the same, the wall cannot last long without cement. Similarly, no work that one does without faith is worth anything to God. Consequently, all works that unbelievers do are worth nothing as far as their well-being [is concerned]. Lady Patience and Lady Strength are the pillars sustaining and supporting the work in such a manner that no wind of tribulation or temptation or destructive words or great sorrow may batter it.

---

[311] Psalm 45:5.

[312] The "city" here represents the conscience, which is the location of the Abbey of the Holy Spirit, as well as the seat of the soul (as in Augustine's *City of God* and the city of the soul in Psalm 46).

[313] God.

[314] Christ's commandment to his disciples before he is betrayed and crucified (John 13:34).

[315] Solomon's temple; 3 Reg. 6. II, par. 3.

[316] Psalm 32:4.

Chapter Four: This speaks of the house, secured by seven pillars, that a noble lady made.

Scripture records that, long ago, one lady made a beautiful and grand manor, and then constructed seven high pillars. But what are these pillars if not the seven virtues: that is to say, faith, hope, love, justice, temperance, fortitude, and prudence? These are the seven pillars by which the abbey, in which the Holy Spirit lives, must be sustained.

Chapter Five: How the cloister of this abbey must be situated and conditioned, and the characteristics and structures of this abbey's offices.

Now it is necessary to make a cloister of the abbey that must have four corners and is called a "cloister" because it must be enclosed and well-guarded. Daughter, if you truly want to be religious, keep yourself closed and shut, and thus guard well your cloister: Lower and close your eyes and abstain from lightly looking; your ears from hearing bad things about others; [close] your mouth from speaking and laughing too much. Close your heart from all evil thoughts.[317] And whoever guards himself well in these four things, certainly he is very religious.

Lady Confession shall make the chapter-house. Lady Prudence shall make the refectory; Orison, the chapel; Contemplation, the dormitory because the dormitory must be high through the removal up of desire,[318] and outside of the strife, tribulation, and worries of this present time. Compassion shall make the infirmary, Devotion the cellar, Meditation the granary because these ladies, that is to say, Compassion, Devotion, and Meditation must be abundant.

Chapter Six: How in this abbey of the Holy Spirit it is necessary to construct a convent; and how God the Father, God the Son, and God the Holy Spirit found it.

---

[317] These four areas of containment (eyes, ears, mouth, heart) represent the four walls of the cloister.

[318] The French here reads "...le dortoir doibt estre hault par soublievement de desire..." (f.3, ll. 26-6). The use of the verb *soulever*, literally "to take up," may be deliberately ambiguous. It can be variously translated as the "the removal of desire" or the "exciting of desire."

Before the officers are thus designated, it is necessary to establish and order the convent with graces and virtues and with the very honored Holy Spirit who is the guard and defender of this religion. So God founds this very noble abbey. And of this, the prophet David says, *Fundauit eam latissimus.*[319] God the Son by his wisdom orders it, as St. Paul says, *Quae sunt a deo ordinatae sunt.*[320] It is, he says, very certain that the abbey and the religion are thus regulated; it is by God the Son ordered, but there also is more: it is the Holy Spirit that is the Guardian, Defender, and Visitor of it. Because of all this, we sing, saying *Veni creator spiritus.*[321] Lord, Holy Spirit, Creator, come, Lord, and so visit the thoughts of those who for love of you will hold the rule of your religion in their hearts and, by your sovereign grace, inspire the pious ones you have created.[322]

Chapter Seven: How Lady Charity was elevated to abbess of this abbey of the Holy Spirit and how all works must be done in Charity.

Before the sweet convent has thus sung and called the Holy Spirit, it needs to have a good abbess and selects Dame Charity because she is valiant and wise, being completely courteous and full of all good habits. And all put themselves completely in obedience because it is like this in religion: one must not do anything, nor go to any place, nor take or give consent without the permission of

---

[319] Psalm 86:5.

[320] Romans 13:1.

[321] A Prayer to the Holy Spirit: "Come Holy Spirit, fill the hearts of Thy faithful and enkindle in them the fire of Thy love./ V: Send forth Thy Spirit and they shall be created./ R: And Thou shalt renew the face of the earth" (The Episcopal Committee of the Confraternity of Christian Doctrine, 2).

[322] The French here reads…: "Sire saint esperit creeur venez sire et si visitez les pensees de ceulz et de celles qui pour lamour de vous tiendront en leurs coeurs la regle de votre religion et par vostre grace souueraine mesprisies les piz ques vous avey creez" (f. 3v, ll. 19-23). This passage appears to be a version of the prayer to the Holy Spirit given in note 321 above. Here, *mesprisies* may be the imperative form of *esprisier* (to value exactly, to appreciate) with an indirect object: *m'esprisiez*. This would translate to "help me appreciate the pious ones you have created." *Esprendre* (to inflame, to inspire) seems particularly appropriate here, although the verb form is not exact. Using *mespriser* (to scorn) necessitates the negation of the phrase for the meaning to be sustained: "…disdain [not] the pious ones you have created."

the abbess. Also the one[323] whom this holy religion and this holy abbey wishes
to guard and establish, he must do nothing and must go to no place nor take or
give anything without the permission of this holy abbess, Madame Charity. And
thus St. Paul commands it, who says, *Omnia vestra in charitate fiant.*[324] You who
wish, he says, to keep and establish this religion in your hearts – that religion
which is well-maintained and often visited, comforted, consoled, and enclosed
by the Holy Spirit – be careful, he says, that all your deeds are done in charity.
Alas, Lord, here is a powerful commandment, but certainly it is good and he who
acts as it commands, saves souls. Great [it] is when he says, "All your thoughts,
your words, your looks, your goings, and your comings and, in brief, all your
deeds whatever they be, do them in charity." Alas, I see some people in religion
do many things, taking and giving, against the advice of Madame Charity.

**Chapter Eight: How Madame Wisdom was elevated in order to be prioress
of the abbey of the Holy Spirit. And Lady Humility is the sub-prioress, and
of all, [there is] none more beautiful.**

Madame Wisdom therefore was elevated in order to be Prioress of the noble
abbey of the Holy Spirit. And this was very right and reasonable because she is
very worthy of it according to that which is written in the book of Solomon where
it says *Prior omnium create est sapiencia.*[325] Know, it says, that Wisdom was created before anything, and by obedience and the counsel of this prioress we must
accomplish all our works if they are to be worth more and be more valued by the
Visitor.[326] And this is what David says: *Omnia in sapiencia fecisti.*[327] So, by this
he wishes to say, "O, you soul that has made Charity the abbess and commander
of your heart and has selected Wisdom so that she might be prioress, you wish to
remain and dwell completely in the obedience and counsel of these two ladies:
Your deeds must be so much better valued and much more dearly held because
of your reverence for these ladies in whose obedience and by whose counsel

---

[323] A novitiate.

[324] I Cor. 16:14.

[325] Eccle. 1:4

[326] The Holy Spirit.

[327] Ps. 103:24.

the [deeds] were done." Madame Humility who always lowers herself and at all times put herself voluntarily at the bottom will be sub-prioress, and it certainly is right [for you] to come to her in obedience for she is well-loved of the Visitor.

Ah, gentle daughter, this is a holy abbey and a good religion where live such valiant people – such saintly, worthy, and capable persons – as the abbess Charity, the prioress Wisdom, and the sub-prioress Humility. Daughter, blessed are the religious who keep well the commandments of Charity, the counsels of Wisdom, and the lessons of Humility, and who will lead, order, and regulate all their lives lovingly, wisely, and humbly. The Father, Son, and Holy Spirit will comfort and aid them, but the people will despise them.[328]

Ah, what a wonder! And yet Jesus Christ says in the gospel to his disciples, "Don't be surprised if the world hates you because it first hated me. If you were of the world, certainly the world would love that which belongs to it. And yet, because you are not of this world, it hates you. Remind yourself," he says, "of the words which I say to you. It is that the sergeant is not more important than the lord because he had said before that the disciple is not more important than his master; nor, therefore, is the sergeant more important than his lord. It must be sufficient for the disciple that he should be as his master and for the young servant that he should be as his lord.[329] If they call the master Beelzebub, as they might wish to, what wonder is it if likewise are called all those [m. & f.] who wish to be his disciples and follow him.

"You know well that I am the lord and master, and that I know and can do all. And you know that before I came on the earth to take on human flesh, all the world was in great misery. For this reason spoke the prophets with very ardent desire, 'Lord, come. Lord, lower your heavens and descend.' And another prophet said, 'He will come, the Lord who is the desire of all people and in all countries.'[330] And many other words these holy fathers said and so petitioned me that I am coming into the world. I bring them peace."

---

[328] The holy "religious" (above).

[329] Matt. 10: 24-5. This passage is also a reference to the Pharisees' accusation of Christ as the prince of demons, Beelzebub, and therefore able to cast out demons. (Matt. 12:24ff, Marc 3:22ff, Luc 11:15ff).

[330] A reference to Old Testament prophesies concerning the birth of Christ, such as that found in Agg. (Aggeus/Haggai) 2:8: "et movebo omnes gentes et veniet desideratus cunctis gentibus et

Chapter Nine: How Jesus Christ our Lord demonstrated here in many ways the great love that he has for us by his coming to the world and by his passion and very cruel death.

"Now, take notice, dear daughter, of the beginning of my life, the middle, and the end, and you will find that it was all [lived] in poverty, tribulation, misfortune, agony, hardship, and in all difficulty. Look now, in what place I was born, with what, not how, I was surrounded, and there where I was put to sleep. Look likewise how the world began early on to hate me and with such a great hatred – that of death. Because of the doubt and hatred that Herod conceived for me, he commanded the death of the Innocents[331] and thought to have killed me among them. Look how my mother transported me to Egypt and from one place to another. Look, still, how I lived sweetly with you in the world. And not for one day or two only but lasting the space of thirty-three years. Look how I taught the world the direct path to eternal life by works and teachings of the mouth because all that I preached there I accomplished by works. Look how the world was never satiated of doing evil to me and how I was never satiated of doing good to them. Look how it converted to evil all the good that I did for it and, to the contrary, how I converted to good all the evil that ever it did to me. And still you may read and find how the world deceived and betrayed me, how it seized me and blasphemed and slapped and spit on me, how it tied me to the column and beat me, [and] then crowned me with thorns.[332] And in the end, after all this, how it condemned me to die, how it crucified me, attaching my feet and hands with large iron spikes to the wooden cross.

Look still, my sweet daughter, that if all the paths and roads that are throughout the world were burdened with cord, and all the fields, plains, hills and valleys were burdened with nails, and with all that I had been tied and nailed, they would not have had any power to hold me one minute against the will of my Father and because of the very great love that I have for you, my dear daughter, and the very

---

implebo domum istam Gloria dicit Dominus exercituum." (And I will move all nations, and the desired of all nations shall come; and I will fill this house with glory, saith the Lord of Hosts.)
[331] The Slaughter of the Innocents, Matt. 2:16-18.
[332] Matt. 26, Mark 14, Luke 22.

great hunger and thirst I have for your well-being. That was the supreme bond that tied me to the column, nailed me to the cross, and suspended me in bonds.

Chapter Ten: How after many beautiful remonstrances, the nuns of the abbey and religion of the Holy Spirit, that is to say, the world, must recognize the great love that Jesus Christ, our Lord, had for us.[333]

"Ah, my very honored and loyal friend, and my very dear redeemer, Jesus Christ, our Lord and Savior of the world, you say the whole, pure truth because I know certainly, very sweet Lord, that no bond whatsoever has ever stopped you at all or restrained you except only the bond of true love and charity which you paid for my disloyalty Certainly, very dear lord, you have been my champion without any conquest and you know, dear Lord, that I have been very seriously diseased and that nothing could give me good health except you and yet to you I could not go. By your great goodness, you came generously to me and you had health and healing for me by your precious blood, the which for my redemption and salvation was spilled in such a manner that the stones and rocks that perceived your death cracked and split so much that they had no need of redemption. Not at all was this blood shed for them.

"But leave me, very sorrowful and miserable, who have very great need of it[334] and for whom it was spilled to my very great profit, [I who] remain completely without splitting, without weakening in anything, and [who] can scarcely feel it. And it is also true that in some way I do feel it, if it is only in passing, and at least to speak of it with difficulty.

Ah, my very honored Redeemer, my God and my Lord, it pleased you by your grace quite benignly to accept a very cruel and horrible death in order to redeem me from eternal death and to give me eternal life. And in this you have shown me the true hawk[335] that killed himself and opened his side in order to give life to his little ones. You know, dear Lord, that my father, the most powerful,

---

[333] *Fille* (Daughter) responds.

[334] Christ's blood, for redemption.

[335] While the French translates literally to "hawk," in most medieval bestiaries this action would be represented by the pelican who rips open its chest to feed its young. The pelican remains a symbol for Christ.

was angered by my great sin and desertion, and menaced me with beating as one who greatly deserved it.[336] But you, very humble and charitable friend, Jesus Christ, who knows my fragility and weakness, certainly have had much pity on me, miserable creature, that you did not have for your very excellent eminence, for to this end the rod of my aforementioned father did not reach itself to me. It pleases you to go and put [yourself] between the two [of us], and there you have received violent blows on the shield of your own, very precious body. By such a manner that shield was suspended and cruelly mutilated in the service of my defense. And you have endured so much abuse and torment for love of me that you had my father completely reconciled to me who, for no one else but you, would have permitted it."

Chapter Eleven: How by the authority of God the Father, Jesus, his Son and Sovereign Judge of humans, all grace and goodness comes to us only from him and by his great loving kindness.

"My very honored Redeemer and very gentle friend, again have you done much too much for me because of the incomparable service that, for love of me, it pleases you to do in presenting yourself and making intercession between my father and me; [it] was so agreeable and pleasing to him that he has pardoned me entirely even though I acted wrongly against him. And what's more, if it comes about that I should again offend him, it would please him that you, very esteemed Lord, be the judge of it, by giving you complete power and authority to judge and condemn everything, as far as I have done wrong.

"Ah, very humble and very merciful Lord Jesus Christ that I might be able to thank you for so many great blessings that up to now you have done for me, because by myself I have nothing except sins and shortcomings. And thus you have completely given me to know how all is yours. And that is right because all things whatsoever truly come and proceed from you, be they blessings of fortune or temporal blessings, riches to have or blessings of nature – such as physical beauty, eloquence, or knowing how to forbear and find one's way among people – or blessings of grace such as are the holy virtues, whoever has them, because all of this comes from you. And such are the gifts that you give by your

---

[336] A possible reference to the beating of the chest in penance while repeating *Mea culpa.*

very noble order that all those [m. & f.] who such blessings have, whoever they are, must hold them from you, not from any other, and not think or believe at all that they possess them [blessings] because of their intelligence, virtue or valor, because one sees very many wise people of great lineage who have been or become poor or uncouth."

Chapter Twelve: How one might anger our lord by being unkind toward the poor who have need and how one must treat them.

"Ah, sweet Lord Jesus Christ, Son of God all powerful, in all things I am cognizant of having greatly transgressed against your very worthy commandments because of the blessings of fortune of which you have made me keeper in order to share them with your creatures who have need of them. And I encountered them [the poor] very distressingly and hid although I was completely aware of their state and how they were my brothers and sisters, and even so, it distressed me to give them five sous out of love and remembrance of you than to dispense twenty sous or more on outrageous things and baubles. And what is worse, this is so very little that I have given for the love of you. I wear myself out, being evil; I have reproach and regret for it many times, so that it seems that it heavily wears me down in such a manner that, by my ingratitude, I have lost the merit of the gift and have made a vice of virtue. Woe is me, a very miserable creature, full of presumption. How much burden I feel from great disloyalty when I know very well my poor brothers and sisters are in very great suffering and misfortune because of poverty. And our Lord generously sent me each day his blessings in order to distribute them and give [them] kindly and lovingly to these [poor people] when they, for the love of God, ask me for it. Those blessings I have retained entirely in order to allot it for my singular profit, the same way that I gave them wickedly very little [while] I pitied them in my ungrateful and unnatural heart.

But leave me, a very wicked sinner. For what enduring use, then, did I have, all my life, so many blessings of fortune and nature that our Lord by his grace sent me in such great abundance? Certainly in no other thing if not in my parentage in which I often prided and glorified myself, and by which I carried and elevated myself more than was appropriate. My natural intelligence and experience I have considered too much, and if I did not expend myself in coming up with and searching for routes and ways by which I might be able to please you, my very honored lord, Jesus Christ, I nevertheless looked for and noticed with all diligence and by many pathways how I might be able to please myself in the world and furnish my body with all worldly pleasures."

Chapter Twelve (*sic*):[337] **How no person should counterfeit more beauty in becoming what nature did not permit, nor attribute to her glory the blessings that came from God to her.**

"Ah, my very sorrowful, ungrateful cadaver limed against the foul odor that after my death soon will begin and surge throughout the pathways of my body which then can be appropriately called a corpse. My beauty that you, my blessed Creator, dispensed to me, was not enough because by great study I thought up and desired many disguises and ways and many diverse and accumulated cosmetic preparations in order to make up and ornament myself, and by these [means], to make my body pale and better comport it so that I should be well-regarded by the world all the time. Certainly, by such feats I have rightly been the damned trickery by which fools and libertines are entertained, by which by chance, and in plain truth, [they] fell into great sin. I am the cause and reason of their damnation in such a manner that these people [m. & f.] cried to you to save themselves, very gentle Jesus Christ, [causing] your precious blood to spill by the aberration of my foolish and very disordered situation. And because of the bad examples I demonstrated before them [m. & f.], I could have put them on the road to eternal damnation. And thus you, most honored Jesus Christ, have given good diligence to save them and all human creatures. I gave up all power [from you] in order to damn eternally them and me. Thus, my stubborn perversity has always been contrary to your estimable goodness."

"As [for] the gifts of the Holy Spirit, thus, of all the graces and virtues and of all the great blessings that without number I have received from you upon the holy fount of baptism, I have certainly polluted all of them and by my iniquity have effectively lost them. And if I did or said anything which yielded or had

---

[337] The numbering of the treatise's chapters becomes inaccurate here, until finally after the last numbered chapter (fourteen, which is in reality number sixteen), the scribe simply indicates the beginning of a new chapter with the words "Le chapitre."

some tinge of good, I wished for it to be praised; therefore, I stole the glory of it from you and appropriated to myself all the honor. If I heard that someone had scorn for you, I took little or no notice, but if someone scorned me or blamed me, I vigorously and openly defended myself against it. If someone praised you and in my presence returned thanks, it was a little thing to me. But if someone praised me in some way for something good I may have done, although I had not myself even done the thing one was praising me for, I accepted the praise for [the deed] without returning it to you, very honored Jesus Christ, from whom all blessings come. In brief, very Sweet Redeemer, Jesus, never did I stop myself from fighting you and being contrary in recompense for all the blessings that all my life, by grace, you have done for me. And all this comes to me by way of great distress for my ingratitude."

Chapter Thirteen (sic): The explication, the lessons, sufferings, and praises that the nuns of this holy abbey and religion must diligently read.

"Ah, leave me, a very unhappy sinner. With what desire would I not wish to have all of this made known when I know that much evil as often come about because of me? Leave [me] until I shall be satiated of doing evil, Lord, when the day and hour of my conversion and emendation will come, when such a great hatred will be able to enter in my heart for all sins for love of you, as for love of me you had hatred for all sins, when you, even you, delivered your precious body to death in order to put sin to death. When will I be able to look on the abyss of my faults with such contempt and hatred that never by any desire would I be able to rise up to do a thing that, my sweet friend Jesus Christ, could turn you to displeasure? When will I be able to have, through you, complete awareness of those blessings which, without number and without measure, I have received from you? How will I not be able to have all true consideration of the very complete love that you continually have had for me? By such things, I might be able to turn about my body, my heart, and all my intentions in order to do the things that would be agreeable to you.

Lord, I see and recognize very well that your reign on earth was disturbed by cruelty and great poverty. And I, by contrast, always wished to lead all my life in riches, honor, and delights. Alas, my very honored and loving Jesus Christ, how has such folly been able to enter and dwell in my heart, which wishes and demands promptly all that which you did not have in this world, by demanding great honors and baubles, there where you, my God, King, and very sovereign Lord died? And concerning the delights [of the world], you had and received there[338] inestimable and innumerable torments. And about desiring the riches of the world, you dwelled there in great poverty.

Certainly, if it came about that the king of France transported himself to some country in his realm and its inhabitants took him prisoner, then allowed him to be tormented and struck, then without any pity, tied and battered him, and finally led him to hang from the gallows without deserving it, those who would do this [we] could not reasonably call devoted and loyal who well knew that their king or lord to have been made to endure and to sustain such very great insult and suffering, and without deserving it at all, to have him so cruelly and inhumanely treated as wrongly to put him to so cruel and villainous a death, tyrannically usurping from him royal honors and ceremonies. Truly, many would hold such people to be foolish and lost.

Alas, my very honored Lord, the same is [true] of us with you, our very good king Jesus Christ, as it is stated above. And all the same must the lessons, praises, sufferings of the religious in this holy abbey and religion be. First, they must read in the psalter of their conscience all their sins and their shortcomings in order to better humble themselves. Afterwards, they must sing of the blessings that the sovereign of the abbey did for them; all of these [blessings] are without number. And how it again promises them that those who well and completely wish to keep all the points of the religion, they shall have in it eternal consolation."

Chapter Fourteen (*sic*): How in the book of Daniel is contained the ordinance of Nebuchadnezzar throughout all his empire in order for life to be led in tranquility.

As said above, one must begin to labor in the valley of his shortcomings and, amid the hope that one has some blessings which belong to his parent, one must climb the mountain of tranquility. This agrees much better [with] that which we read in the book of Daniel where he says that a great king who had the name

---

[338] In the world.

Nebuchadnezzar, King of Babylon, established through his entire realm three men who governed and ordered everything there for the benefit of the common-weal, and in such a manner that Nebuchadnezzar had neither disruption of any progress nor any discord or quarrel in his palace. Thus, his estate and life were guided by Peace, Consolation, and Tranquility. Similarly, it happens in the spiritual realm of the Holy Spirit in which there are three directors. And the religious where these three prelates are established shall not have complaints or quarrels but [instead] joy and peace. And blessed be the realm and the religion which is made and ordered by Charity and Humility.

Chapter Fourteen (*sic*): How four ladies, that is, Discretion, Oroison,[339] Devotion, and Penitence, have duties in the Abbey of the Holy Spirit.

[Along] with all offices stated above, Lady Discretion is established in the Abbey of the Holy Spirit as the treasurer who guards all and occupies herself so that all goes just as it should. Lady Praise is the chanter[340] and raises the chants of the day and night in order to praise God, and Jubilation is her companion. St Gregory said that Jubilation is a very great joy which is conceived in tears through love and by the favor of the Spirit which can neither be completely shown nor completely hidden. It sometimes comes to spiritual people after prayers which are so joyous and with consolation so ardent that their hearts go singing and murmuring a song throughout their hall and among their chambers, where it sometimes happens that the tongue does not know how to consider that which it sings.

Another lady, Devotion, is overseer of the cellar who has in her keeping the white and rose wines as roses and flowers of remembrance of God, our Redeemer, and of his very holy Passion and of his very great goodness and glorious company in Paradise. And Lady Penitence does the cooking because she takes enough care. For satisfaction,[341] she prepares and makes the food good and often dry by contrition, and she eats little because of abstinence. And Mademoiselle Temperance is the keeper of the cold room who in exercising her office serves so carefully that no one shall have too much to eat or drink. Lady

---

[339] Praise.

[340] Song leader.

[341] Of sins.

Sobriety reads at the table the lives of the Holy Fathers and sings to them [the religious] in their ears how they [the Holy Fathers] previously overcame, by this exhorting them throughout the convent to do likewise in order to take from there a good example.

Lady Pity is the keeper of the pittance and very diligently visits the sick in administering all their needs to them, to each person according to his station. Misericord,[342] her sister, is the almoner who gives so much that not much remains with her. Madame Fear is the porter who guards very well the cloister of the conscience by rejecting evil and calling in the good so that no wickedness may enter within the cloister of the heart and conscience through the doors of the mouth, ears, or eyes which are all windows that we do well to guard night and day. Lady Honesty is guard of the novices and teaches them to speak to the point and to go in an honest and saintly manner so that all who see them can take a good example [from them].

And this is that which the apostle admonishes us saying, *honeste ambulemus.*[343] Let us comport ourselves, he says, honestly.

And Lady Courtesy must certainly be the innkeeper in order to receive properly those who come, in such a manner that all [m. & f.] may be able to praise her for it. But since a religious must not be alone among those who arrive [while she is] exercising the office of innkeeper, to this end – that she might not be too joyous or too liberal with her company – Lady Courtesy shall have a companion named Lady Simplicity, because they are very good together and worth little without one another. Consider that too great a simplicity would be considered foolish while too great a courtesy would be too joyous and bold, but the two together serve well and beautifully.

Madame Reason is purveyor because she provides within and without and in such a way that no fault at all is found there.

Lady Loyalty is the keeper of the infirmary because she loyally works to serve the sick. And especially since there are more of the sick and weak than [there are] of the strong and healthy, Lady Largess is, therefore, her companion who administers throughout because she worries herself little about the great expenditures that she makes in order to provide for the good and welfare of the sick and suffering.

---

[342] Mercy
[343] Rom. 13:13.

Madame Meditation, who is very prudent and wise, is keeper of the granary and assembles the good wheat and the other good grains in plenty, to the end that in their sustenance there will not be any lack. Certainly Meditation is a virtue that one calls thinking well of our Lord God and of all his deeds and his words equally. King David very much loved this keeper of the granary [Meditation] and for this reason he was rich all his life and in plenty, of which it says in the psalter, *Et meditabor in omnibus operibus tuis.* "Lord," says he, "I think of all your deeds." And again he says, *Meditatus sum in omnibus operibus tuis in factis manuum tuarum meditabar.*[344] "Lord," he says, "I think of all your deeds and I think of the works of your hands." And he says again that those are truly happy who contemplate the law of God day and night. And this is the beginning of perfection when gladly one begins to think of our Lord very intentionally because it is completely thus that the fruit is worth more than the leaf. Thus, much better is a good thought in holy meditation than many words in prayer.

But I touch again too high and tell you that when a good and devout heart is first elevated in prayer, it is able to say nothing, rather [it] has so much to do in thinking of what it hears, what it feels, and what it sees that it lacks words. It quiets itself in order to learn better to cry out and to speak. And thus, David, the psalmist, says, *Quoniam tacui dum...clamarem tota die.*[345] "I quiet myself," says he, "to this end: that to God I might cry."

The gloss says that the great cries that we cry to our Lord are the great desires that we have from God. And Saint Denis says that when a heart is drunk with a great desire of love, truly, it cannot speak well of that which it feels; rather it is so amazed and stunned that, frankly, it lacks words. And this is appropriately called Holy Meditation that keeps the grains of wheat which are reddish on the outside and white on the inside, and are split in the side. And from such wheat one made the good and savory bread by which is signified Jesus Christ, our Lord, because he says to us, "I am the Bread of Life," because his very worthy humanity was red from his very precious blood in his Passion, and certainly his soul was all white through purity and innocence, and it was by the spear

---

[344] Ps. 142:5.
[345] Ps. 31:3.

that Longinus wounded [him] in the side.[346] This bread we take in the very holy sacrament of the Host.

And Saint Augustine spoke of Meditation when he said, "Lord, when I think of the great sweetness honeyed by the sweetest honey, if all those who see you, in desiring you, see me and I don't see any of them, if they would all be converted by the inestimable blessings that you did for me, the virtuous and great delights [would be] so much, without comparison. And see here the very good keeper of the grain. Now you must know that the granary is and must be before the cellar and similarly, Meditation must come before Devotion. And, consequently, I say that Meditation is the keeper of the granary and Devotion is the keeper of the cellar. And Lady Pity is the keeper of the pittance. And David, the psalmist, says of these three ladies, A fructu frumenti vini et olei sui multiplicati sunt. "These three places," he says, "are multiplied by the fruit of the grain, wine, and oil."[347]

Chapter:[348] How our Lord in the bible promises to those who serve him well an abundance of fruit, that is, his permanent glory.

In many places in the Bible, our Lord makes this promise, saying, "Serve me well and truly I shall give you a great abundance of wheat." This abundance of wheat is given by contemplation of the cross and of the Passion of Jesus Christ,

---

[346] According to tradition, Longinus is the name of the soldier who wounded Christ in the side with his sword at the crucifixion. The lance of the Grail legend is sometimes identified as that of Longinus, or Longeus as he is known in Mallory. (See Vinaver's edition of Mallory's works, p. 54). As a mystical experience, the mythical spear of Longinus links with the Holy Grail tradition (which names the Grail as the cup in which Christ's blood was caught at the crucifixion) because it causes the original drops to fall from Christ's side. The thrusting of the sword upward toward the heart in medieval representations as that found in folio 18v of *The Rothschild Canticles*, according to Lori Walters, represents a direct communion with Christ, a mystical state of union. Much as in *The Canticles* where sexual images are interpreted as spiritual symbols, the sword, which originates in images of sexual vigor and fertility, becomes imbued with connotations of spirituality and mysticism. See R.S. Loomis, *Arthurian Literature in the Middle Ages*; Norris J. Lacy and Geoffrey Ashe, *The Arthurian Handbook,* and Lori Walters, "The Tournai *Rose* as a Secular and a Sacred Epithalamium."

[347] Grain, wine, and oil also reference the Host and wine of the Eucharist, and the holy oil used for administering the holy rites of the Church.

[348] See fn.330, p. 142.

our Redeemer. And this is Meditation. The abundance of wine comes about by greatly crying and meditating, and this is Devotion. An abundance of oil comes from delighting oneself well in our Lord, and this is consolation, because oil gives much good taste and shines in the church, burning in the lamp, similarly, a heart when it has well thought and well adored him [Christ], God has compassion on it and gives it comfort, pity, and delight.

First, [God] sends him the sweet wheat of Meditation; afterward, [he] gives him the wine of Devotion. Then, [he] imparts to him the oil of pity and consolation, and this oil gives savor and affection, and illumines by knowledge and revelation, and burns by the fervor of natural inflammation.

A very wise lady who is called Jealousy and who is always awake in order to do good, keeps and governs the time-piece to wake all the others and to get them up in the morning in order to serve our Lord. In the good towns are timekeepers that wake the countrymen and these are the roosters that wake themselves up by their own nature before the day and most of their morning, their song giving knowledge to the countrymen that morning is approaching. And elsewhere in the cities are other timekeepers that wake the citizens and merchants, and these are the watchmen who trumpet the crack of dawn. But there is another kind of time-keeper in this religion and holy place of devotion that Lady Jealousy governs by the savor of perfection. And because of this, it happens many times in religion that before the sound of the time-piece for matins, devout people have cried tears in great abundance out of love and devotion before the representation of the Lord because the time-piece of love had awakened them.

Chapter: How the heart of everyone must keep awake in great jealousy, diligence, and desire, through the love of our Lord.

Ah, Daughter, blessed be the soul that complete love diligently awakes, that is not at all asleep or slothful, and thus we have ourselves read in the book of the Canticles, *Ego dormio et cor meum vigillat.* That is to say, when I sleep physically and recline in order to rest my body a little, my heart is continually awake in jealousy, in burning love and desire for God. Such a soul always has its understanding and heart focused on its honored Creator so that it is able to sing a worldly song, saying, "I have a heart awakened to songs of love."

The songs of the heart are the yearnings, sighs, misgivings, groans, and desires that the holy soul has continually in its prayers.

Chapter: How the enemy of hell put in the Abbey of the Holy Spirit four of his daughters: that is, Envy, Pride/Presumption, Murmur/Detraction, and False Judgment of Others.

Before this noble abbey was perfected and ordered as said, and our Lord was highly and well served and honored by great study and good diligence, one great usurer of the peace (made so much by his manner of acting and malice) put there his four daughters who were very ugly. But who was this malicious usurer? Truly, this was the enemy from hell. The first of his daughters was named Envy who is so cross-eyed and squinting that she was not able to see straight but always sideways as is evident in Saul and David. The second daughter was called Pride/Presumption who is so hunch-backed and swollen in the chest that it was amazing because she believed herself to know more and be worth more than the others, as is shown in Naaman. The third called herself Murmur/Detraction because truly she is so stammering that she knew not how to speak either well or beautifully; rather she is always the lady of tension and quarrel, and sows discord throughout the religion. The fourth had the name of False Judgment of Others, and this daughter is so lame that she cannot go right and also thinks of nothing good, neither of loyalty nor of truth.

Chapter: How by prayer the aforementioned four daughters of the enemy of hell were thrown out of the abbey of the Holy Spirit.

The four daughters of the usurer mentioned above, who by malice were put in the notable abbey of the Holy Spirit, troubled all of the convent in such a manner that all went badly. That is why the religious of the convent – Madame Charity, the abbess; Madame Sapience, the prioress; Madame Humility, the sub-prioress; and all the other good ladies – in seeing this [trouble] roused themselves and sounded the chapter. Then they counseled themselves in order to know what they should do. Then Madame Discretion counseled them diligently that they should go pray, beseeching the very sweet Holy Spirit so that he by his grace might come save them because they were in very great need.

And then with great devotion, they sang *Veni creator spiritus.*[349] This they did immediately with great vigor. The Holy Spirit arrived to them, who by his grace and eminence threw out of his abbey these four daughters of the devil, that is Pride/Presumption, Envy, False Judgment of Others, and Murmur/Detraction, as false, evil, filthy harlots unworthy to ever live as honest people because they always valued too greatly the very worst company.

The end and conclusion of this present treaty entitled *The Abbey of the Holy Ghost.*

Then was the noble abbey of the Holy Spirit reformed and [made] new, much more ordered than it had been before.

Now, I pray you all [m. &f.] who this holy religion wish to keep, be as diligent as you [m. & f.] can be so that each of these good ladies named in this present treaty will know daily their spiritual duty in your hearts. And guard yourselves well so that you do not trespass the rule of the religion nor the obedience of the sovereigns, at all. And if it should happen by some mischance that any of the aforementioned four daughters of the enemy from hell fight in your hearts, act on the counsel of Madame Discretion and immediately recover in prayer, calling with very ardent desire on the very honored Holy Spirit who, as a very humble and all-charitable Visitor, will immediately come and eject from you all filth. In such a manner, the convent of your conscience will remain peaceable and virtuous because your conscience shall be the temple of the blessed Holy Spirit. So be it. Amen.

Here ends the book entitled *The Abbey of the Holy Ghost.*

---

[349] A sung prayer to the Holy Spirit.

BIBLIOGRAPHY

Manuscripts Containing English texts
of *The Abbey of the Holy Ghost*

Add. Ms. 22283. British Library. London.

Add. Ms. 36983. British Library. London.

Bradford-Lawrence Ms. 8. Fitzwilliam Museum.

Egerton Ms. 3245. British Library. London.

Eng. Poet Ms. A.1. Bodleian Library. London.

Harley Ms. 1704. British Library. London.

Harley Ms. 2406. British Library. London.

Harley Ms. 5272. British Library. London.

Lambeth Ms. 432. Lambeth Palace.

Laud Misc. Ms. 210. Bodleian Library. Oxford.

Ms. 155. Corpus Christi College. Oxford.

Ms. A.5.2. Lincoln Cathedral. Lincoln.

Ms. Dd.XI.89. Cambridge University Library. Cambridge.

Ms.Ll.V.18. Cambridge University Library. Cambridge.

Ms.Ii.IV.9. Cambridge University Library. Cambridge.

Ms.Q.1.29. Trinity College. Cambridge.

Ms.Q.D.4. Jesus College. Cambridge.

Ms. Chandos-Pole-Gell. Keio University, Tokyo.

Ms. Douce 141. Bodleian Library. Oxford.

Ms. Douce 323. Bodleian Library. Oxford.

Peniarth Ms. 334. National Library. Wales.

Stonyhurst College Ms. B.XXIII. Stonyhurst College. Lancaster.

Winchester College Ms. 33. Fellows Library. Winchester.

Manuscripts Containing French Texts
of *L'Abbaye du saint esprit*

Add. Ms. 20697. British Library. London.

Add. Ms. 29986. British Library. London.

BNF 2095. La Bibliothèque Nationale de France. Paris.

BNF 19397. La Bibliothèque Nationale de France. Paris.

Ms. Arsenal 3167. La Bibliothèque de l'Arsenal, Paris.

Ms. Bibliothèque Royale 9555-58. Bruxelles.

Ms. Douce 365. Bodleian Library, Oxford.

Ms. Nouv. Acq. Fr. 5232. La Bibliothèque Nationale de France. Paris.

Ms. Vesoul 91. La Bibliothèque Nationale de France. Paris.

Royale 16E.XII. British Library. London.

Yates Thompson Ms. 11. British Library. London.

Related, Unpublished French Treatise

Le Dialogue de la Duchesse de Burgogne à Jésu Christ. Add. 7970. British Library.

Published Sources

Allen, Hope Emily. *Writings Ascribed to Richard Rolle, Hermit of Hampole, and Materials for His Biography.* New York: Heath, 1927.

Allen, Rosamund. "Introduction." *Richard Rolle: The English Writings.* New York: Paulist Press, 1988.

Barber, Richard. *The Pastons: A Family in the Wars of the Roses.* Woodbridge: Boydell, 1986.

Blake, N.F., Trans. *Middle English Religious Prose.* London: Billing & Sons, 1972.

Blockmans, Wims. "The Devotion of a Lonely Duchess." *Margaret of York, Simon Marion, and* The Visions of Tondal. Ed. Thomas Kren. Malibu: Getty Museum, 1992.

Blumenfeld-Kosinski, Renate. *Poets, Saints, and Visionaries of the Great Schism, 1378-1417.* University Park: Penn State U P, 2006.

Boffey, Julia. "*The Charter of the Abbey of the Holy Ghost* and Its Role in Manuscript Anthologies." *The Yearbook of English Studies*: 33 (2003), 120-130.

Brown. Review. *Speculum*: 71.3 (1996), 1033.

Buhler, Curt F. "The First Edition of "The Abbey of the Holy Ghost." *Studies in Bibliography:* 6 (1953-54), 101-06.

Bynum, Carolyn Walker. *Jesus as Mother.* Berkley: U of California P, 1982.

—. *Metamorphosis and Identity.* New York, 2001.

Carruthers, Mary. *The Book of Memory.* Cambridge, Cambridge U P, 1990.

The Catalogue of Additions to the Manuscripts in the British Museum, 1854-1860. London: The Trustees of the British Museum, 1965.

The Catalogue of Additions to the Manuscripts of the British Library, 1876-1881. London: Trustees of the British Museum, 1967.

The Catalogue of Western Manuscripts in the Old Royal and King's Collections. London: Trustees of the British Museum. 1921.

The Charter of the Abbey of the Holy Ghost: A Critical Edition from All Known Extant Manuscripts with Introduction, Notes, and Glossary. Ed. Clara Elizabeth Fanning. Diss. Fordham, 1975. Ann Arbor: UMI, 1975.

Chase, Steven. *Contemplation and Compassion.* Maryknoll, NY: Orbis, 2003.

Chastellain, G. *Oeuvres.* Ed. Kervyn de Littenhove. *Académie royal de Belgique*: V. 249-278.

Chesney, Kathleen. "Notes on Some Treatises of Devotion Intended for Margaret of York (Ms. Douce 365)." *Medium Aevum*: 20 (1951), 11-39.

Consacro, Peter. *The Author of* The Abbey of the Holy Ghost *from All Known Extant English Manuscripts with Introduction, Notes, and Glossary.* Diss. Fordham, 1971. Ann Arbor: UMI, 1971.

De Mazilles, Jehan in Commynes-Dupont, *Preuves*, III. 241-242.

De Winter, Patrick. "The *Grandes Heures* of Philip the Bold, Duke of Burgundy: The Copyist Jean L'Avenant and His Patrons at the French Court." *Speculum* 57(1982).4.

Duffy, Eamon. *The Stripping of the Altars: Traditional Religion in England, 1400-1580.* New Haven: Yale U P, 2005.

Fanning, Clara Elizabeth. *The Charter of the Abbey of the Holy Ghost: A Critical Edition from All Known Extant Manuscripts with Introduction, Notes, and Glossary.* Diss. Fordham, 1975. Ann Arbor: UMI, 1975.

Giuliano, Paula. "Introduction." *The Mystery of the Passion of the Third Day.* Asheville, N C: 1996.

Gregory the Great. *Moralium libri epistula missoria*: III PL, LXXV, 513C.

Grote, Geert. "Letter 23." *Gerardi Magni Epistolae.* Ed. W. Mulder. Antwerp, 1933.

Gunn, Steven. "Henry VII and Charles the Bold: Brothers under the Skin?" *History Today*: 46.4 (1996), 28.

Hamburger, Jeffrey. *Nuns as Artists: The Visual Culture of a Medieval Convent.* New York: U of California P, 1997.

—. *The Visual and the Visionary: Art and Female Spirituality in Late Medieval Germany.* New York: Zone Books, 1998.

Horstmann, C. *Yorkshire Writers: Richard Rolle of Hampole and His Followers.* London: Swan Sonnenschein, 1895.

Hugh of St. Victor. *The Didascalicon of Hugh of Saint Victor.* Trans. Jerome Taylor. New York: Columbia U P, 1991.

—. *Fundamental Writings.* Vol. 2. Trans. Member of CSMV. USA: Revelation Insight, 2009.

Jaouen, Françoise and Benjamin Semple, Eds. "Editor's Preface: The Body into Text." Yale French Studies 86 (1994).

Lacy, Norris J. and Geoffrey Ashe. *The Arthurian Handbook.* New York: Routledge, 1997.

Lambert, Malcolm. *Medieval Heresy: Popular Movements from the Gregorian Reform to the Reformation.* Malden, MA: Blackwell, 2002.

Lawrence, C.H. *Medieval Monasticism.* London: Longman, 2001.

Loomis, R.S. *Arthurian Literature in the Middle Ages.* Oxford: Clarendon P, 1974.

Madan, Falconer. *A Summary of Western Manuscripts in the Bodleian Library at Oxford.* Oxford: Clarendon P, 1897.

McGann, Jerome. *A Critique of Modern Textual Criticism.* Chicago: U of Chicago P, 1985.

—. "The Monks and the Giants," *Textual Criticism and Literary Interpretation.* Chicago: U of Chicago P, 1985.

McGrady, Deborah. *Controlling Readers: Guillaume de Machaut and His Late Medieval Audience.* Buffalo: U of Toronto P, 2006.

McNamara, Jo Ann. "Sexual Equality and the Cult of Virginity in Early Christian Thought." *Feminist Studies*: 3.3/4 (1976), 145-158.

Mews, Constant, Ed. *Listen Daughter.* New York: Palgrave, 2001.

Meyer, Paul. "Notice du Ms. Royal 16E.XII du Musée Britannique." *Bulletin de la Société des anciens textes Français*: 38(1912), 45-63.

Morgan, Nigel. "Texts of Devotion and Religious Instruction Associated with Margaret of York." *Margaret of York, Simon Marmion, and* The Visions of Tondal. Ed. Thomas Kren. Malibu: J. Paul Getty Museum, 1992.

Quilligan, Maureen. *The Allegory of Female Authority.* Ithaca: Cornell U P, 1991.

Pinder, Janice. "Love and Reason from Hugh of Fouilloy to the *Abbaye du saint esprit*: Changes at the Top in the Medieval Cloister Allegory." *Parergon* 27 (2010), 67-83.

—. "The Cloister and the Garden." *Listen, Daughter.* Ed. Constant Mews. New York: Palgrave, 2001.

Rice, Nicole R. "Spiritual Ambition and the Translation of the Cloister: *The Abbey* and *Charter of the Holy Ghost.*" *Viator: Medieval and Renaissance Studies*: 33 (2002), 222-260.

Savage, Ann and Nicholas Watson. Introduction to *"Sawles Warde." Anchoritic Spirituality: Ancrene Wisse and Associated Works.* New York: Paulist P, 1991.

Simons, Walter. *Cities of Ladies: Beguine Communities in the Medieval Low Countries, 1200-1565.* Philadelphia: U of Penn P, 2003.

Smalley, Beryl. *The Study of the Bible in the Middle Ages.* New York: Philosophical Library, 1952.

Stamler, W. *Prosa der deutschen Gotik: Eine Stilge Schichte in Texten.* Berlin: Cat. No. 28. 1933.

Sur la Terre comme au ciel: Jardins d'Occident á la fin du Moyen Age. Ed. Elisabeth Antoine. Paris: Musées nationaux, 2002.

Taylor, Aline. *Isabel of Burgundy.* New York: Tempus, 2002.

Theilemans, M.R. "Introduction." *Marguerite d'York et son temps*. Brussels: Banque de Bruxelles, 1967.

Theological Glossary. *The New Jerusalem Bible*. Henry Wansbrough, Ed. New York: Doubleday, 1990.

Van Engen, John. *Devotio Moderna: Basic Writings*. Classics of Western Spirituality. New York: Paulist P, 1988.

Vaughan, Richard. *Charles the Bold: The Last Valois Duke of Burgundy*. New York: Boydell, 2002.

Vinaver, Eugene. *Malory's Complete Works*. Oxford: Oxford U P, 1977.

The Visions of Tondal. Trans. Madeleine McDermott and Roger S. Wieck. Malibu, 1990.

Walters, Lori. "The Royal Vernacular: Poet and Patron in Christine de Pizan's *Charles V* and the *Sept psaumes allégorisés*." *The Vernacular Spirit: Essays on Medieval Religious Literature*. Eds., Renate Blumenfeld_Kosinski, Duncan Robertson, and Nancy Bradley Warren. New York, 2002.

—. "The Tournai *Rose* as a Secular and a Sacred Epithalamium." *The Court and Cultural Diversity*. Eds. Evelyn Mullaly and John Thompson. Cambridge: D.S. Brewer, 1997. 251-66.

Warren, Nancy Bradley. *The Embodied Word: Female Spiritualities, Contested Orthodoxies, and English Religious Cultures, 1350-1700*. Notre Dame: U of Notre Dame P, 2010.

Weightman, Christine. *Margaret of York: Duchess of Burgundy, 1446-1503*. New York: St. Martin's P, 1989.

Whitehead, Christiana. "Making a Cloister of the Soul in Medieval Religious Treatises." *Medium Aevum*. 67 (1998): 1-29.

ACKNOWLEDGMENTS

This book finds its origins in research undertaken to fulfill requirements for a doctorate in Medieval Literature from Florida State University. Consequently, I would especially like to thank members of my doctoral committee who guided me, giving generously of their time and expertise: Dr. Eugene Crook (Chairman), Dr. Lori Walters, Dr. David Johnston, Dr. Helen Burke, and Dr. Marcie North. While continuing to research the topic in subsequent years, I have received kind assistance from staff at the British Library, the Bodleian Library at Oxford University, and the Bibliothèque Nationale de France. In addition to these research professionals, Sue Garis, Margaret Hall, Dorinda Apgar, Robert Apgar, and Linda Moore have spent much time proofreading my work and commenting on possible oversights. Encouragement has also come from a wider circle of friends whose support has personally meant a great deal, as well as from opportunities to share ideas at conferences and through workshops given at Kanuga, North Carolina, and in Tallahassee, Florida.

In addition to these good people, I would like to thank sincerely the person who has been steadfastly enthusiastic and supportive of my work – my husband, Richard A. Hall – to whom, together with our family, this book is lovingly dedicated.

ABOUT THE AUTHOR

Dr. Kathryn Anderson Hall is a Medievalist who currently writes, lectures, and gives workshops on aspects of medieval literature, especially that literature concerning the medieval mystics and saints of the Church. She holds a Ph.D. in Medieval Literature from Florida State University as well as Master's and Bachelor's degrees from Virginia Tech. While working with variations of *The Abbey of the Holy Ghost* in Old and Middle French as well as in Middle English manuscripts, she became interested in the medieval mystics, especially the women of that era who experienced their spirituality through bodily and emotional experiences.

She has served as an Instructor and as an Adjunct Professor of English at Florida State University, taught as a Medievalist in the English Department at Valdosta State University in Georgia, and currently teaches Medieval Literature classes, contractually, for Florida State University's Osher Lifelong Learning Institute (OLLI). In addition, Dr. Hall gives lectures and leads workshops on the medieval Christian mystics for private groups, upon request.

Her writings have been published in *The Sixteenth Century Journal.* XLIII.1 (2012): 284-285; *Studies in Medieval and Renaissance Teaching.* 18.2 (Fall 2011): 59-78; *The South Atlantic Review.* 72.4 (2008): 59-71; and *Contexts and Continuities: Proceedings of the IVth International Colloquium on Christine de Pizan,* Glasgow: University of Glasgow Press, 2002.